F**K BUSINESS

DISCARDED

F**K BUSINESS

THE BUSINESS OF BREXIT

IAIN ANDERSON

Biteback Publishing

First published in Great Britain in 2019 by
Biteback Publishing Ltd
Westminster Tower
3 Albert Embankment
London SE1 7SP
Copyright © Iain Anderson 2019

ISBN 978-1-78590-532-2

10 9 8 7 6 5 4 3 2 1

A CIP catalogue record for this book is available from the British Library.

Set in Minion Pro

Printed and bound in Great Britain by
CPI Group (UK) Ltd, Croydon CR0 4YY

MIX
Paper from
responsible sources
FSC® C020471
FSC
www.fsc.org

To my family – this is actually what I do
To Mark – thank you for being my rock
To my Cicero Group colleagues – this is your story

CONTENTS

PREFACE

In late June 2018 I was attempting to enjoy a peaceful week-end away from Brexit and the business of lobbying – which is my business – but instead I awoke to blaring headlines about the latest zesty soundbite from the then Foreign Secretary. He had been reported by the *Daily Telegraph* as railing against business and its lobbying efforts to secure a good deal with the EU. He was said to have snorted: 'Fuck business,' in an off-the-cuff remark to a diplomat who decided to ring up the papers and decry the comment.[1]

I don't like expletives at the best of times, I don't like using them myself and I especially don't like Cabinet ministers using them to depict their attitude towards business and wealth creators – but I felt the title of this book wrote itself! Expletives appear to be the *noms du jour* – they cut through the imagination and serve up headlines in the current age of populism where 'plaster may fall off the ceiling' on to the lexicon of politics. I agonised about putting them on the

---

1   James Crisp, Peter Foster and Gordon Rayner, 'EU diplomats shocked by Boris's "four-letter reply" to business concerns about Brexit', *Daily Telegraph*, 23 June 2018.

front cover of this book. But I want them to arrest the senses. Something has gone badly wrong in our discourse.

Those two words summed up the disconnect between our political leaders and our leading businessmen and women, which has been growing for years. It wasn't just the sentiments of our new Prime Minister but an attitude which is widely held.

I waited to hear a retraction or denial from his entourage, but I waited in vain. So, I emailed the chairman of one of the UK's biggest FTSE 100 companies and also one of the leading business trade bodies and said I thought a clear response was needed. They agreed.

I then got in touch with Henry Zeffman at *The Times*. He asked for a Red Box daily briefing comment as soon as possible. 'If it's punchy enough, it will make a news story,' said Henry. I told him: 'Don't worry – it will be.'

But the outburst provoked wider thoughts. What had gone wrong in the relationship between business and politics? As someone who is a passionate advocate of the need for policymakers and businesspeople to work together for a common good, I believe we have been living through the worst of times. The financial crisis over a decade ago eroded trust between our politicians and business folk, and events since have only served to make things a lot worse.

Of course, it's true that not every business leader opposed Brexit. Far from it. Many have been strong proponents of the idea. In this book I will talk to both sides of the argument. I backed Remain but have been on record many times to say our country needs to move on and make the best of the result of the 2016 referendum. We can't keep going around in circles. Far from being a 'Remoaner', I have worked constantly in the past three years to try to improve the dialogue between business and politicians.

Since the referendum, most business leaders have become resigned to it and want to break into a new economic and political cycle. They have not signed up to endless referendums. But everyone – leaders of both large and small entities, and including myself – wanted a positive 'deal' with the EU to secure a transition towards the 'new world' outside the union. When the blog site BrexitCentral launched in September 2016, I was one of its first contributors and found myself compelled to indicate that, while I had backed Remain, I was also a democrat and that we needed to leave the EU in a way that created economic opportunity not damage.

Three years after the referendum, it has been very difficult to review those words today. Opportunities have been lost and the country appears more divided than ever.

As head of the UK's biggest independent lobbying company, Cicero Group, it's my job to translate politics for businesspeople, as well as the other way around. It has given me a ringside seat on our politics, sitting alongside many of the most important businesses in our country. Often those businesses are foreign-owned, by people who view our politics from afar while investing billions in jobs and infrastructure in the UK and who need more translation than most. Many of them remain utterly dumbfounded by the disconnect between politics and business.

Recently I spent an entire day with a Swiss national who has become a leading CEO of a major UK business charting the breakdown in relations. He was perplexed by the UK political situation and knew just how tough negotiations with the EU had been for Switzerland in recent times. My history lesson to the Swiss CEO began in the late 1960s, when I was born, when Enoch Powell started his fight against globalising trends with his 'Rivers of Blood' intervention in 1968, which was to poison Tory thinking for years to come. It set in train two clearly distinct schools of thought within the governing Conservative Party: one open to markets and internationalism; the other deeply sceptical of change and global influences.

I will admit that this book has been cathartic for me. Through the maelstrom of events in the past few years it aims to unpack what's gone wrong by analysing the critical events leading up to the Brexit referendum and its aftermath. Unashamedly, it looks at the relationship in particular between the City and our politicians, for it is the City where I have spent most of my time during my career, firstly as a financial journalist and later as lobbyist. The discussions I have had during my career – the meetings between finance and politics that I have sat in; the understanding that I gained – have all shaped my thinking.

This book also draws on my thirty-five years as a member of the Conservative Party and looks at the relationship between the Tories (which have always been viewed as the 'natural party of business') and commerce – an alliance which became eroded through the thirteen years of Labour government under Blair and Brown.

The book takes us through the coalition to the 'dry run' for Brexit in the Scottish independence poll in 2014 and goes on to look in some depth at the EU referendum and its aftermath, including the travails of the May administration and its wary relations with business. I recall personal stories of friendships on all sides of politics and enterprise, and of the view from my ringside seat with business leaders, the UK's main regulators and the political decision makers and their advisers. It ends just at the time when Boris Johnson – the man whose quote gave the book its name – has been revealed as the man who will be attempting to steer us through the next stages in the Brexit saga.

I come to the conclusion that so much has been 'lost in translation' between the political class and our wealth creators that many on both sides don't really understand each other any more – and perhaps don't want to. However, a new chapter has opened in British politics with a new Prime Minister. I have a genuine hope that things can only get better. Perhaps the relationship with business and politics can be rebooted – or, even better, remade.

From a semi-autobiographical perspective, this book offers a peek into the world of business engagement with the political class. It is built upon my direct experiences over the past decade and more, alongside new and exclusive interviews for this book carried out with some of the country's leading economic and political players as the high drama of the Brexit endgame unfolded in the spring and summer of 2019.

This book is not intended to be an academic 'tome' or a political philosophy textbook but an easily readable account of the period which lifts the lid on the relationship between business and politics right now. It does not attempt to offer a political treatise or make policy conclusions, but I hope to tell the story of how business and politics have grown apart.

Our wonderful team at Cicero Group has been an inspiration during this period, attempting to halve the divide between the political class and our major economic players. We have had many successes along the way, but I stop writing this book at a time when it has never been more important to try to rekindle the relationships once again.

I never thought I would write a book, but I felt compelled to do so. All the mistakes in this effort are entirely mine, but I could not have completed this project without my brilliant researcher and Cicero colleague Omar Rana and my long-standing support and personal assistant Kerensa Grant. To them, I offer my enduring thanks. The team at my publisher Biteback, led by James Stephens and my fantastic editor Olivia Beattie, and her colleagues Ellen Heaney and Suzanne Sangster, have made this project a personal joy – and helped make the words better than I ever could myself.

None of my work would be possible without the love, support and guidance of my husband Mark Twigg and my parents, to whom this book is partly dedicated.

From all these thoughts and experiences, I just hope there are lessons to be learned for both sides. This book attempts to draw the history of the business of Brexit.

I

PARTY GAMES

For most of my adult life – certainly until the past decade – the Tory Party prided itself on being the party of business. For large and small business, and domestic and international firms, you could always depend on the centre right in Britain to be better disposed to the wealth creators, whoever they were. However, over the course of the past few years the stable relationship between the Conservative Party and business has steadily broken down, with the EU referendum of 2016 unleashing an even faster decline in those relations for many business leaders.

The Thatcher government told an intensely pro-enterprise story. Most business leaders warmed to Maggie's desire to unleash capitalism, seen in everything from her major reforms to the City to opening up the UK economy towards competitive forces. The door of No. 10 was open to business, and unashamedly so; business felt it had a place at the table. Of course, some history books of the 1980s would suggest that those same competitive forces unleashed economic effects that led to social division, creating the long-term conditions necessary for the 'howl' against traditional politics that the Brexit referendum represented.

During John Major's administration, his Chancellor Ken Clarke's concern was to bring the economy back from the brink of the ERM crisis in 1992. At that time, you could always find a friendly face leaning in towards businesspeople in the form of the Tory Party, who would remain in power until their crushing defeat in 1997 to Blair.

Let's be honest, that friendly smile was often predicated on the need for the Conservatives to bankroll themselves by contributions from captains of industry while Labour looked to their union barons – although that may be a little unfair. Those captains were motivated by pro-enterprise policies that – most of the time – Labour could not (or would not) meet.

But our more recent history has upended all that. Probably the most striking impact on this landscape was the arrival of Tony Blair as Labour leader in 1994. His repudiation of the long-standing Clause IV mantra of state ownership as one of the earliest acts of his leadership in April 1995, combined with the Tories' deep unpopularity among the broader electorate in the late 1990s, changed the zeitgeist.

Tony Blair, Gordon Brown, Peter Mandelson and Alistair Darling bounced around a 'rubber chicken' circuit of corporate events to woo business suitors. It worked. Businesses sensed that the Tories were going out of power. They were tired and their reputation for economic competence – in my view, still the primary driver of politics – was shot. From Richard Branson to the private equity magnate Ronald Cohen, many wealth creators supported Blair and Brown in their droves and partied till dawn at New Labour's triumphant victory celebration at Royal Festival Hall in May 1997, ushering in the longest period of Labour government ever. Of course, everyone likes a winner, and with its most pro-business agenda ever New Labour scooped up support that was to abandon the Tories for two more electoral 'waves'.

Years later, on the night of 23 June 2016, I was to be at the Royal Festival Hall myself for the Remain 'victory' celebrations. By 1 a.m., however, when the voters of Sunderland opined on our destiny, there was not much to celebrate. New Labour types mingled with the Cameroon class. Of course, that was precisely the problem for the 'elites', and the Brexit referendum showed it up. A new zeitgeist had emerged in our politics. Margaret Thatcher's blue-collar Tory vote, which economically and politically had morphed into New Labour's 'Mondeo man', was now exemplified by the workers of Nissan in Sunderland. Despite being told by all the 'expert' economic analysis that leaving the EU might put jobs at risk, they had voted Out. 'Take back control' – unsupported by any of the mainstream parties and major business leaders – had done its job. Identity trumped economics.

For most of the ten years from 1997 until the financial crash, New Labour continued to court business. Mandelson boasted that he had no problem with businesspeople becoming 'filthy rich'. New Labour pursued a pro-enterprise ethos and, in the end, tax-lowering policies for business. London became a magnet for global finance and Labour Chancellor Gordon Brown didn't even blush when he opened the new European headquarters of Goldman Sachs in the heart of the City of London. With some strange irony, Goldman's took over the former *Daily Telegraph* building in Fleet Street; what a metaphor for the change in sentiment. There was no doubting that it gave Brown a spring in his step and a glint in his eye.

For the Tories, over the long years while Labour kept winning elections with massive majorities, the sense that a 'global corporate elite' had abandoned them continued to grow, festering even among many Tory activists. On top of this, big business had started to abandon direct engagement with the Conservatives themselves. I remember attending the Conservative conference in my day job as a lobbyist in 2003. OK, I admit I have been attending Tory conferences since the infamous 1984 Brighton bombing, when I was barely sixteen, but the 2003 event was perhaps the nadir of Tory fortunes, with Iain Duncan Smith receiving around eighteen rather manically organised standing ovations to show to the watching nation how the faithful loved the 'dear leader'. The conference had the look of a small sect who had gathered to fanatically applaud a most ill-suited political leader. It was fantasyland for most businesses; it was a fantasy for people in the hall, too. Within weeks, IDS was gone.

While the 'quiet man' declared he was 'turning up the volume', most businesspeople had not bothered to turn on their TVs to watch. The usual highly expensive, party coffer-filling trade exhibition stands from Britain's major firms were nowhere to be seen. You could buy a fetching silk tie from a very nice chap running a small stand, or talk to the Conservative Trade Unionists at their stand – but where were the FTSE 100s queuing up to pay £35,000 for four days with the Tories? Nowhere to be seen.

Of course, as a lobbyist, I know that business always wants to flirt with power. Convincing the corporate elite to turn up at a party conference with a party that was – at that time – almost seven years away from being back in power may not be a good use of resources and time.

But the Tories noticed. The thousands of Tory members who did turn up found themselves in a new kind of bubble – one that was further and further removed from that corporate elite.

Like a divorce in which both sides have stopped talking to each other and are only communicating through third parties, the mistrust and lack of understanding simply grew. It would take another general election and a global financial crisis to change things.

Many Tories were and remain brilliant entrepreneurs, lots of whom run small and medium-sized enterprises (SMEs). It's what makes them Conservatives. However, a sense of 'them and us' grew: the Tory entrepreneurs versus the New Labour corporatists, you might call it. At just that time – and I saw this as a lobbyist – the 'corporates' started to engage with and lobby directly with the EU on a truly massive scale. It was where the really big decisions were being taken for many of our major economic players, especially the City. Until even the early 2000s, when I launched my own entrepreneurial venture (a lobbying business working mainly with those corporates), most UK firms, unlike their French, German or Italian counterparts, had not really taken the idea of talking to the European Parliament or Commission seriously. While the UK had been part of the European Community since 1973, UK businesses, like our political class, had been reluctant Europeans.

The EU's Lisbon Agenda in 2000 changed all that. Here was a plan to create a deep, integrated single market. At once the banks, pharmaceutical companies, insurers, tech firms, logistics business, food manufacturers and car makers embraced the feeling. They could see an opportunity to tap the

EU market in a more seamless way and expand their reach. For many international firms who had located in the UK, being able to 'passport' their products and services into the EU was set to be a major growth opportunity.

By the first decade of the twenty-first century, Britain's major businesses – and those who had located in the UK to passport into the EU – had exploited the 'just-in-time' nature of complicated pan-European supply chains. The City of London was becoming deeply interlinked with European business as the leading capital market of the EU. For example, Lufthansa and BMW chose London above other EU locations to raise capital.

The leaders of commerce felt more European than ever. And they also welcomed the Blair–Brown government's embrace of open EU migration to drive forward their corporate ambitions and their bottom line. Europe was proving to be a major economic opportunity. For US business in particular, locating their EU hub in the UK made sense, as language and cultural kinship was a great starting point. London boomed as a result, but the gap between the capital and the rest of the country became a chasm.

Back in 2001, I had worked hard to get Ken Clarke elected as Conservative leader. It was Ken's second attempt. Against all expectations and without a background in economics, he had been widely acknowledged as a brilliant Chancellor under Major, picking up the reins in 1993 following the disastrous ERM crisis the following year, and had gifted the spoils of a positive economic trajectory to his successor, Gordon Brown. Brown kept to Clarke's fiscal targets for much of his own first term as Chancellor before opening up the spending taps.

The following story encapsulates the distance the Tory Party had travelled on Europe since the days of Ted Heath having a majority of Tory MPs and members enthusiastically in favour of European Community membership, or its applauding when Margaret Thatcher championed the Single European Act 1986, which laid the foundation for the single market. Ken's problem in the party was his overt and unspinnable enthusiasm for the EU. I often reflect that in the 1970s and early 1980s, with his charisma, intellect and ability to connect with most people, he would probably have walked a leadership contest. But times were very different in Toryland. In some ways, Ken is like Boris. He speaks without spin, has the ability to connect with people outside politics and is known best by his first name. Of course, the similarity ends there. Boris better caught the mood of his party on the major issue of our times.

At his first attempt, during the 1997 Tory leadership election – the last one to be undertaken only by Conservative MPs, without a ballot of the membership at large – Ken Clarke gained 45 per cent of the vote to William Hague's 55 per cent. When thinking back about Hague, you can't help but feel he won the Tory leadership at precisely the wrong time. In 1997, Ken's candidacy was about closing the gap with Labour. I believed that he could best Blair as a heavyweight at Prime Minister's Questions and, of course, he would have roundly opposed the decision to go to war in Iraq. He would have given the Tories a clearer point of difference.

By 2001, when Hague was spent as leader after an election campaign trying to 'save the pound', the Tories were thrust into a fresh leadership election. I was at Ken's side for much of the campaign, ferrying him to speak to Tory members

across the country. By this time, Conservatives were rede-
fining themselves from 'members' into 'activists'. This defi-
nition was fundamental, as it signified a different kind of
political engagement with the party, where the individual's
voice in politics becomes just as important as the viewpoint
offered from the leadership. 'Members' had grown frustrated
for decades, sat in their constituency associations, that the
Westminster elite were not listening to them. Hague's decision to change the Tory leadership rules meant that all party
members would get a vote on their new leader for the first
time. They were 'activated' in every sense. The party was
transformed from the one I had known, with its deferential
acquiescence to the leadership.

The 2001 leadership campaign was very hard work and it
was to provide further understanding of the increasing EU
scepticism within the party. Ken's decision to share a pro-EU
platform with the 'hated' Blair in October 1999 was continually brought up as a 'traitorous' event by members in meeting
after meeting. But rather than keep quiet about his pro-EU
views, Ken couldn't be tempted away from his enthusiasm.
It was the most infuriating yet joyous thing about him – his
unspinnable qualities! He was and remains a politician that
the media love because of exactly that approach.

In the middle of the 2001 leadership campaign, *Newsnight*
organised the first ever TV debate between two contenders to
become a party leader, to be chaired by Jeremy Vine. It seems
amazing to think now that was the first ever televised leadership debate. I – along with Ken's campaign manager, the forensic future Treasury Select Committee chair Andrew Tyrie MP
(a self-described EU sceptic of the time), and communications

chief Richard Chalk – prepared Ken for the debate in his enormous corner offices at Portcullis House above Westminster Tube, which had, given his seniority in the House, one of the best views of the river Thames in all of Westminster.

Ken didn't keep the most orderly of offices, but he could lay his hands on everything with the help of his longstanding assistant Debbie Sugg. Sitting amid deep mounds of parliamentary papers piled up across his office on every spare flat surface, we told Ken to move the debate away from Europe; we would never, ever, beat Iain Duncan Smith with the Tory faithful in the country on that subject. We told Ken: 'Talk about transport, health, education, the police or housing. Anything but Europe. You won't win.' He nodded and said: 'Don't worry – I've got it.'

So Richard, Ken and I got into the car and drove off to the former BBC TV Centre in Shepherd's Bush, west London. Ken was greeted by the producer, and Richard and I were ushered into the *Newsnight* green room, which had been prepared for us as Ken's team. IDS's entourage had another room to use.

Like the teams behind prizefighters in this newest of political dramas, we were to remain in our own corners. The BBC had supplied a bottle of red wine for the guests, but the runner (the person who gets guests to the right place) indicated it might not be of the best quality. Richard and I waved Ken off to make-up and we both resolved not to touch a drop. We had endured a long week of campaigning, and another early start beckoned the next day, so we opted for the hot drinks on offer. Brewing a cup of tea, we sat back to watch the debate. The familiar *Newsnight* titles and music rolled. Jeremy Vine introduced the contenders. Ken looked to be in sparkling form with his trademark 'twinkle' in his eye. IDS – as ever – looked ill-suited to being on the telly.

After the initial verbal blows at each other, I could see Ken gesturing to Jeremy Vine. 'Yes, Ken?' said Jeremy, slightly unsure of the new format the BBC had unleashed on him. Ken smiled broadly. 'I don't think there's anybody more Eurosceptic in the Conservative Party than Iain.' Richard Chalk and I looked at each other and just knew the rest of the debate would be dominated by the issue of Europe. Richard and I shrugged and opened the screw-top bottle of BBC red. By the end of the 45-minute debate there was none left.

Ken lost the Tory leadership poll in 2001 under the new voting system by 39 per cent to IDS's 61 per cent. By 2005, when Ken – the standard bearer for the pro-Europeans in the party – stood for a third time, he didn't even make it to the final two. The gravitational pull of Euroscepticism had done its work.

In fact, in order to get elected as leader against his run-off opponent, the much more Eurosceptic David Davis, in 2005, David Cameron had to promise to take the Tories out of the centre-right grouping in the EU Parliament, the European People's Party (EPP). It was that decision – a commitment made in 2005 that no one remembered by 2009 – that cut the Conservatives fully adrift from their own place at the heart of the European centre-right conversation. Of course, inside the Conservative Party, the argument was continually made that the EPP was fully in line with the 'federalist' project of the EU to achieve deeper economic and social integration. But that was never completely the case inside the EPP, and the desertion of the UK Conservatives served only to intensify that tendency. One Tory MP told me: 'All we did was to cut ourselves off even more from the decision making of the EU's biggest political grouping just as it was calling all the shots in the EU. It was crazy.'

Many businesses looked on mystified and bewildered that, just as they had begun playing an even greater part in Europe, the Conservatives continued to drift further away from it. By the late 2000s, some of the business folk who had abandoned the Tories in 1997 had started to drift back. They could see that Labour was tiring and in Cameron the Tories had a young, energetic leader. Early supporters, like City veteran Michael Spencer, also brought backers to the table again. Business scented that the Conservatives were coming back into power and wanted to get close again. But when they did re-engage, they found a very different grassroots party to the one which had left power in 1997. As a result, a very different and far more Eurosceptic group of candidates was set to get elected to Parliament in 2010.

The financial crash, which started with the unravelling of the sub-prime mortgage crisis, hastened more business back. Cameron's easy style and his embrace of a social liberalism appealed to many of them. When Brown 'bottled it' and failed to call a general election in autumn 2007 before the financial crisis really hit home for most voters, Cameron and Osborne saw their chance. At the Tory conference that same year, Osborne unveiled a package of reforms slashing inheritance tax and capital gains which, by its very design, appealed to ordinary homeowners who had seen the value of their homes mushroom in the Brown 'boom' only to trap many of them and their older relatives in high taxation. At the same time, business owners could see a new pro-enterprise agenda set against a tiring Labour Party.

Watching the BBC *Ten O'Clock News* on Monday 1 October 2007 from my Blackpool hotel room (the best way to enjoy any conference and do some work at the same time), I saw the Tories' new policies lead the bulletin, with a report from political editor Nick Robinson focusing on shadow Chancellor George Osborne's conference speech for a full ten minutes. The Conservatives had not dominated the news agenda in this way since leaving power a decade earlier.

This was to be the last time one of the major parties was to go to Blackpool for its conference. Cameron had seized the Tory crown in Blackpool two years earlier with his electrifying 'no-notes' hustings speech. Unlike for IDS back in 2003, Blackpool had proved to be better for Cameron and Osborne's fortunes – and their relationships with business. The Tories were back in earnest. The money followed. The lobbying of the Tory front bench intensified. Business flocked back to their annual conferences. It looked like Cameron would be in Downing Street by May 2010.

Business knew the Tories had moved into a deeply Eurosceptic place over the previous decade, but Cameron had promised them that his party would stop 'banging on about Europe'. When in power, commerce thought he would be able to curtail the anti-EU sentiments. For a time, that was true. Following the 2010 election, when Cameron had to enter a coalition agreement with Nick Clegg – leader of the UK's most EU-friendly party – most businesses thought the problem had gone away. Clegg would be the brake on the Tory Euroscepticism. And he was – but not for long.

2

THE ROAD TO BLOOMBERG

After the Blair and Brown years ended with the financial crash, business was very happy to see a Tory-led government back in power. The 'natural party of government' and of business seemed to have found its stride once again. The so-called socially liberal 'corporate elite' was also pretty pleased to see David Cameron enter into a deal with Nick Clegg's Liberal Democrats. Clegg would provide a buffer against the Euroscepticism around the Cabinet table and on the green benches in Parliament.

Centrist politics is where most modern business leaders – many of them with their MBAs and business school gongs – had been. Maybe that's where business always is; with one eye on its own 'liberal' education and life experience, and another on its customers, whom it doesn't want to 'offend' in any way, it takes a middle-of-the-road approach. So the deal between Cameron and Clegg did not disappoint. The coalition agreement looked to focus on fiscal recovery from the crash alongside a series of policies which would drive social integration. It ruled out a massive upheaval in our relationship with the EU by barely mentioning it. On the issue of EU membership, there wasn't even a debate at the top of British business. The consensus was clearly: 'It's a good thing,' and most firms exploited the opportunities of the single market and open EU immigration to the max.

The modus operandi of the Cameron government was to open the door to business. The massive outreach that had taken place in opposition by Cameron and Osborne continued into government. Both knew that the Tories banging on about Europe for the previous decade had been one of the main reasons for business leaders to support New Labour. So, they set out to change the tune – and they used Nick Clegg as the perfect excuse to say to their own party and, privately, to business leaders: 'Our coalition partners just won't wear a referendum.' This line was repeated again and again to business leaders. When, in May 2013, one of Cameron's inner circle referred to UKIP supporters and the most Eurosceptic members of his own party as 'swivel-eyed loons', his reference was met with quiet nods from business. Of course – as I have already argued – most of the business elite didn't spend time with the 'loons' to find out why they thought what they did about the EU. Business chiefs spent time with other business chiefs or with those at the very top of the political machine. Not with Tory constituency activists, nor with UKIP either.

On top of that, a whole bunch of new Tory MPs had been elected in 2010 who had moved the parliamentary party much further towards Euroscepticism. The previous decade had seen a hardening of attitudes against the EU among the 'selectorate' of Tory constituency associations that pick the candidates to run with a blue rosette. Candidly, this is the reason I never put myself forward as a candidate myself, despite my long association with Conservative politics. I just didn't think my brand of Conservatism would pass the test of the selectorate.

In early 2010, before the election, the influential ConservativeHome website ran a conference in Westminster specifically designed to appeal to corporate lobbyists. The room was packed. The website's creator, Tim Montgomerie, and his team provided an incisive 'insider' analysis of the likely make-up of the new Conservative parliamentary party, but I think most people in the room believed that Cameron as Prime Minister would push back against the Eurosceptics. As Montgomerie commented later, in 2011, when discussing the Eurosceptic members of the new intake of Tory MPs: 'By sheer volume – accounting for half of the parliamentary party and two thirds of Tory backbenchers – they will pull Cameron towards more Thatcherite positions.'[2]

Despite the coalition promising to get on with reducing the deficit as its core priority, there was growing sentiment building for a vote on Britain's membership of the EU. In 2011, the House of Commons rejected an EU referendum motion by a vote of 483 to 111. The vote had been provoked after a public petition received more than 100,000 votes. However, showing the growing tide of opinion in Conservative politics, the vote was the worst Conservative rebellion on Europe ever seen, with eighty-one backbench MPs voting against the government. John Major's troubles with his Maastricht 'bastards' were as nothing compared to this outbreak. Most of them were indeed Eurosceptics, but there were one or two (likely the newly elected Robin Walker, who

---

2   Tim Montgomerie, 'The Class of 2010 is reshaping the Tory Party for the Better', *Daily Telegraph*, 25 June 2011.

in the end campaigned for Remain in 2016 and also became the longest-standing DExEU minister under May) who just wanted to see the issue finally put to bed in a people's vote.

To placate his Eurosceptic MPs, Prime Minister Cameron said that he supported the aims of fundamentally changing the UK's relationship with the EU.

> Like you, I want to see fundamental reform. Like you, I want to re-fashion our membership of the EU so that it better serves our nation's interests. The time for reform is coming. That is the prize. Let us not be distracted from seizing it. I commend this statement to the House.[3]

Many in business shuddered. They had thought that Cameron had meant what he said about closing down the subject under his premiership. Despite his party's EU obsession, he had promised this would not be an issue. They thought the civil service would help close the matter and fill ministers' red boxes with other things to do. But from that point on Eurosceptic Conservative MPs' approach to the Europe question would be to demand ever more reform in UK–EU relations, responding not just to their constituency associations but also to the growing drumbeat of Eurosceptic politics led by UKIP, which was eating away at Tory support. This challenge set an unfeasibly high bar for the Prime Minister to reach – one he would ultimately fail to achieve.

The day before the vote on the referendum motion, the Tory grassroots blog site ConservativeHome – now read as much by

---

3   Hansard, HC Deb, 24 October 2011, vol. 534, col. 27.

the lobby media and lobbyists as Tory Party members themselves – published polling figures which suggested that 72 per cent of Conservative members favoured a second referendum. Fired up with that level of support, former Cabinet minister John Redwood MP, the long-standing Eurosceptic, opined:

> The heart of the Conservative Party is Eurosceptic. Last night more showed their heart. Many of the remaining Conservatives who voted No did so whilst … saying they wanted less EU government and wanted a referendum at some other time. The drum beat of the Conservative party is to renegotiate. It is to get a new relationship with Euroland. The party is united in this. It speaks for the overwhelming majority of the UK electorate.[4]

Foreseeing the debate in the Tory Party some five years later, when Cameron would return from Brussels with his EU referendum 'deal', James Forsyth, *The Spectator*'s political editor and perhaps the Cameron No. 10 machine's closest confidant among the lobby, wrote:

> This should be a wake-up call to David Cameron. He needs to develop a proper policy for repatriating powers from Brussels, change his style of party management, and reform the Whips office. This rebellion will encourage the hard-line Euro-sceptics to try again and again. They will reckon, rightly, that as the parliament goes on the number of potential rebels will grow. If they can get this number of rebels in year two

---

4   John Redwood, 'More voices than votes', JohnRedwoodsDiary.com, 25 October 2011.

of the parliament, imagine how many they'll attract in 2014 when a whole bunch more MPs have been passed over for promotion. The idea that this vote has lanced the boil or dealt with the issue of Europe for the parliament is for the birds.[5]

Later that year, Cameron anticipated that he needed to show his Eurosceptic party he was serious about confronting the EU. In a high-stakes late-night drama in Brussels, he vetoed an EU-wide treaty amendment which was intended to provide a solution to the eurozone crisis. The change had been designed to keep the EU project on the road. Concocted in Brussels, it was portrayed as a way of showing EU-wide 'solidarity' – a much-used phrase which may have resonance in the corridors of power in Paris and Berlin but falls flat when conveyed to readers of the *Daily Telegraph* and the *Daily Mail*. The proposed amendment to the Lisbon Treaty would have enacted the following:

- A cap of 0.5 per cent of GDP on countries' annual structural deficits.
- 'Automatic consequences' for countries in which the public deficit exceeds 3 per cent of GDP.
- Tighter fiscal rules to be enshrined in countries' constitutions.
- A European Stability Mechanism (ESM) to be accelerated and brought into force in July 2012.
- A reassessment of the adequacy of the €500 billion limit for the ESM.

5   Quoted in BBC News Daily View, 'What now for Britain in Europe', Clare Spencer, 25 October 2011.

- The eurozone and other EU countries would be required to provide up to €200 billion to the IMF to help debt-stricken eurozone members.

Cameron said:

> We want the eurozone countries to come together and solve their problems. But we should only allow that to happen within the EU treaties if there are proper protections for the single market, for other key British interests. Without those safeguards it is better not to have a treaty within a treaty, but have those countries make their arrangements separately.[6]

The main reason for David Cameron's veto was that it contained insufficient protections for the UK's financial services industry. In public, the City was pleased that Cameron had gone in to bat for them, but in private, even my friends in the financial services sector could see that he had weakened the UK's standing across the EU. This treaty change was an attempt to create more fiscal rectitude in the EU's approach, and Cameron had blown it up. Right-of-centre EU leaders like Merkel were dumbfounded.

Speaking to me for this book, the chair of one of the UK's biggest banks said:

> I noted that the relations between the UK Treasury team and their Brussels counterparts – which had been excellent

---

6   Nicholas Watt, 'Eurozone countries go it alone with new treaty that excludes Britain', *The Guardian*, 9 December 2011.

for years – became seriously eroded at this point. They were never to recover and I think that had its own effect at the end of this decade when the Treasury did not do any heavy lifting for financial services during the Brexit negotiations.

So, back in December 2011, despite the EU scepticism, the question was: why would a centre-right leader not support a 'sound money' package to secure the eurozone and prevent economic contagion across Europe spilling into the UK economy? I think the answer remains in how the 'veto' would be portrayed on the UK political scene. It was the first real sign that Cameron wanted a 'win' with the EU. It may have damaged relations with Brussels, but the *Daily Mail* did indeed love it, running the headline 'The Day PM put Britain first' and suggesting: 'Business Backs Cameron Veto'. However, the City and the rest of business was applauding through gritted teeth. They could see he had sown the seeds of EU resentment. The business team at No. 10 reached out to get industry leaders to cheerlead for Cameron, but privately business was telling Brussels something entirely different in their lobbying. Business had wanted to see the EU debt crisis put to bed, but Cameron had just stirred it up, at the same time creating tensions that would ultimately make it all the harder to secure a good deal to convince voters to back Remain. In December 2011, Britain appeared to be in splendid isolation.

To tell that story of that 'gritted-teeth' reaction from business, let's look at some of the rather equivocal comments of the time in reaction to his move. Reporting on the business divide between those who wanted further EU reform to be achieved and those who sought to ensure the UK did not become more isolated, the *Financial Times* quoted the following:

> Georg Grodzki, head of credit research at Legal & General: 'The pressure and rush to arrive at consensus was undue. Other EU leaders should not be surprised not to get what they want.'
>
> Mark Burgess, chief investment officer at Threadneedle Asset Management: 'Financial services are a much greater part of the economy than in other EU economies, and the financial transaction tax would have been very damaging to the UK.'
>
> Angela Knight, chief executive of the British Bankers' Association and former Tory HM Treasury Minister under John Major: 'Europe has given us a framework for what to do tomorrow, but not the way for how we are going to get from today to tomorrow. The big thing for what to do about today's uncertainty has still not been achieved.'

So yes, in public, the City was highly supportive of the Prime Minister. However, in private, fears abounded that the UK was cutting itself off from the heart of the EU conversation. Having dropped membership of the European People's Party in 2009, the Tories were no longer caucusing with Merkel and Sarkozy. The ability to sort out differences on a party basis 'off the table' of the EU summits was no longer an option for either side.

At this time, I saw major business organisations like the Confederation of British Industry (CBI) and Federation of Small Businesses (FSB), as well as the largest UK firms and

inward investors in the UK, significantly increase their lobbying firepower in Brussels. There was a growing sense that
UK businesses and those international firms who used the
UK as their passport into the EU would need to 'talk over
the heads of' the British government and get directly to the
decision makers in Brussels. This did nothing to build trust
with the Tories.

They had been building presence in Brussels for some time,
but the lobbying spend (especially from the City, which had
been dealing with a raft of legislation in the aftermath of the
financial crisis) went through the roof. Cameron's splendid
isolation was not going to be an option for business. So, despite the promises from Cameron two years earlier, 2012 was
to be characterised by 'banging on about Europe'.

The House of Commons referendum vote in 2011 and the
move by Cameron at the end of 2011 at the EU summit had
only intensified the debate and provided fuel for UKIP. The
growing momentum behind the anti-EU party was eating
into Conservative support, and Cameron knew it. Something
had to be done. But how to cauterise the wound? After weeks
of expectation, on 23 January 2013 David Cameron delivered
a speech at the iconic Bloomberg European headquarters in
London, where he pledged to renegotiate the UK's relationship with the EU and put that changed membership package
in an in/out referendum after the next general election and
by the end of 2017.

The weeks leading up to the speech involved Cameron's
Europe minister, David Lidington, engaging in the Hercule-
an task of shuttling back and forward to Brussels and Berlin
and testing which notes to chime. He spent more time in

Berlin, as the UK had calculated that getting a good response from Merkel was key to the entire enterprise.

Cameron believed that by offering a referendum he could put the political problem to bed, both for the Tories and for business. The plain fact was that he never believed he would have to make good on the commitment. The No. 10 business outreach team went into overdrive, and I found myself being given a 'test drive' of elements of the package to try out with some major businesses. Most CEOs could see why Cameron needed to do something, but they feared he was opening Pandora's Box.

I remember calling long-standing friends and relatively new Tory MPs Robert Buckland and Liz Truss – two MPs sitting on opposite ends of the spectrum in the EU drama – to piece together how the speech would play with the parliamentary party. They had both entered Parliament in 2010 and were seen as ones to watch. Both said to me that Cameron had probably done enough in his speech for now, but they agreed that it was only going to grow as a problem. Bloomberg was to be the start of the next chapter in the story, not an end point.

At Cicero, in order to better understand the underlying issues behind a political event, we often draft 'client notes'; you will read a lot more about this technique throughout the book. The purpose of the notes is a little like that of papers produced by City analysts. They are designed to unpack fundamental issues – in this case, the unfolding politics – and provide business with a deeper understanding of the drivers of events and attempt to form conclusions about the way ahead. It's not lobbying, as they are not about a specific political 'ask'. They are more about political risk analysis, to help clients factor the politics into their decisions. I drafted a client note at the time, warning business there was much more to come as a result of the Cameron Bloomberg speech.

I remember tuning in to watch the speech and spotting many of the captains of the businesses I worked with in the audience. I've been listening to political speeches for most of my life. Cameron was on top form and spoke passionately about the need for the UK to remain at the heart of the EU but to attempt to achieve a new settlement with Europe. Nevertheless, he left plenty of questions hanging. Most importantly, while he spoke about his belief that the UK was destined to stay and play a part in the EU's journey, he studiously avoided saying how he would campaign in any vote. Guided by the belief that he would need to renegotiate, he sat on the fence and did not make the case for Remain. Business and the wider world watching on were entreated to believe that David Cameron himself could get a better deal with the EU. The conclusion to my note to clients back in 2013 was that Cameron was placing himself front and centre for the campaign ahead.

Given its importance to Cameron's strategy with his party and with the EU, it's worth laying out in some depth here exactly what he said in the Bloomberg speech:

Just as I believe that Britain should want to remain in the EU so the EU should want us to stay.

For an EU without Britain, without one of Europe's strongest powers, a country which in many ways invented the single market, and which brings real heft to Europe's influence on the world stage, which plays by the rules and which is a force for liberal economic reform, would be a very different kind of European Union.

And it is hard to argue that the EU would not be greatly diminished by Britain's departure …

I know there will be those who say the vision I have outlined will be impossible to achieve. That there is no way our partners will cooperate. That the British people have set themselves on a path to inevitable exit. And that if we aren't comfortable being in the EU after forty years, we never will be.

But I refuse to take such a defeatist attitude – either for Britain or for Europe.

Because with courage and conviction I believe we can deliver a more flexible, adaptable and open European Union in which the interests and ambitions of all its members can be met.

With courage and conviction I believe we can achieve a new settlement in which Britain can be comfortable and all our countries can thrive.[7]

After he finished, I called and emailed everyone from major investors to the business representative organisations. The mood was one of cautious optimism, though one business leader said to me: 'The genie is out of the bottle now and it's going to be very difficult to put it back in.'

The wider political reaction was swift. Labour leader Ed Miliband said:

---

7   David Cameron, 'EU Speech at Bloomberg', www.gov.uk.

Why can't he say unequivocally that he's for Yes in a referendum? Because he's frightened of the people behind him. The only thing that's changed is that a few months ago, when he said he was against an in/out referendum, is not the situation in Europe, it's the situation in the Tory Party.[8]

Cameron's coalition partner and Deputy Prime Minister Nick Clegg provided some cover:

Of course, there is the right time and the right place for a referendum. In fact, it's this coalition government, Liberal Democrats and Conservatives, who've put in law for the first time a guarantee to the British people of the circumstances in which a referendum will take place. But we should always be governed by what's in the national interest. My view is that years and years of uncertainty because of a protracted, ill-defined renegotiation of our place in Europe is not in the national interest because it hits growth and jobs.[9]

At the time I put pen to electronic paper myself in a blog for the Huffington Post:

THE UK MUST REMAIN AT THE EU TABLE – THE PM IS RIGHT
If you were at all unsure about David Cameron's commitment on IN or OUT of the EU – you only needed to listen or read some of the Prime Minister's closing words in this

---

8 'David Cameron speech: UK and the EU', BBC News, 23 January 2013.
9 Ibid.

most hyped of speeches. 'If we left the EU it would be a one-way ticket – not a return.'

He could not have been clearer as he talked constantly of his view that the UK must remain 'at the table' to be able to influence its decisions. He made continued reference to the single market as a prime mover in the UK's economic interests...

The emphasis on the single market will particularly please business and inward investors who see the UK as the platform for EU investment. The kind of deal the Government struck on banking union in December 2012 is exactly what most businesses I talk to want to see.[10]

Business organisations tried to be as supportive as they could while recognising that Cameron had unleashed something that they could not control. The British Chambers of Commerce said:

Announcing plans for a referendum on British membership puts the onus on the rest of Europe to take the Prime Minister seriously, as they will now see that he is prepared to walk away from the table. But the lengthy timescale for negotiation and referendum must be shortened, with the aim of securing a cross-party consensus and the outline of a deal during this Parliament.

The CBI – the UK's biggest business body, which was to have a loud voice in the Brexit debate ahead – commented:

---

10 Iain Anderson, 'The UK Must Remain at the EU Table – the PM is Right', The Blog, HuffPost, 23 January 2013.

The EU single market is fundamental to Britain's future economic success, but the closer union of the eurozone is not for us. The prime minister rightly recognises the benefits of retaining membership of what must be a reformed EU and the CBI will work closely with government to get the best deal for Britain.

The Institute of Directors, representing individual company directors, had been at the peak of its powers under Thatcher but had been steadily reinventing itself as a champion of corporate governance and the new economy. Led by the charismatic former No. 10 insider Simon Walker, it also weighed in on the debate, saying: 'A future referendum to decide the workings of our relationship is the best way to affirm Britain's participation in a free-market Europe which is competitive and deregulated.'[11]

Around the time of the speech, I received a call from Matthew Elliott. He had been the master campaigner on the alternative vote referendum in 2011, and not long afterwards I rather informally asked if he would like to become a lobbyist; Matthew very politely declined. More the brilliant campaigner than the corporate lobbyist, Matthew had secured a huge victory for No to AV in the first referendum of Cameron's tenure. He had also been the driving force behind the creation of the TaxPayers' Alliance, a lobbying group which sought to expose government waste. The alliance was supported by a group of individuals and highly nimble business leaders who would mostly define themselves as 'entrepreneurs' rather than 'corporates'.

---

11 BBC News, 'David Cameron speech: UK and the EU', 23 January 2013.

Matthew invited me and a couple of other senior lobbyists to come and join him for a meeting in Westminster to talk about the referendum campaign ahead. He knew I had worked for Ken Clarke as well as with those corporates who had seen the EU single market and passport as a huge driver of their growth, but he encouraged me to join. I think he was keen to have a broad tent of support for his ambitions, or at least to smoke out my personal intentions and those of my clients in the likely battles ahead.

Intrigued, I wanted to discover – at the very least – what his own ambitions were. Matthew had been referenced constantly in the newspapers at the time as someone who might be joining Cameron in No. 10. This was something he always denied, but his brilliance at campaigning was known to Osborne and the Prime Minister and I know that they wanted him to be on their side when the time came. The fact that Elliott decided to plough his own furrow rather than join Cameron will rank as one of the key turning points in the unfolding Brexit drama.

I headed down to Westminster to meet Elliott in the offices of the communications and lobbying headhunters Ellwood Atfield at 34 Smith Square in the heart of SW1. The meeting room was next door to the former Conservative Central Office which had become famous as the scene of Thatcher's three election victory celebrations. It was now – irony of ironies – the home of the EU Commission in London! The spacious Ellwood Atfield room is often hired out to host meetings of all kinds of political and corporate forums, but for some years it has also played host to a gallery of political pictures and a wonderful series of political cartoons from across the ages. I sat down to meet with Elliott surrounded by pictures of our politics past and present.

In a very short presentation – clarity and brevity are one of Matthew Elliott's great hallmarks – he laid out a prospectus which was to build the 'For Britain' campaign. It would be bankrolled by major donors but was to set in train grassroots impact. He talked of 'Bikers for Britain', 'Builders for Britain', 'Sports stars for Britain' and, most importantly – for me and for those in the room that day – 'Business for Britain'. He was laying out to us what would eventually become the architecture of the Vote Leave operation and the business backing it would need to cultivate in order to ensure it had broad-based support. Sensing this, I had to ask a question: 'Is this not just the starting point for the Leave campaign?' His answer was instructive. 'Not necessarily,' he replied. 'This work is designed to strengthen the Prime Minister's hand in the forthcoming renegotiations.'

'You know where I come from here, Matthew,' I replied. 'The vast majority of business I work with want to stay in the EU. I am personally also committed to that.' He acknowledged the point but asked me to take a look at the campaigning materials when they launched in a few weeks' time and to reserve judgement until then. I said I would.

True to his word and working quickly, Matthew made sure a draft letter to the newspapers arrived in my inbox within days. It called for all political parties to promise a referendum on Britain's membership of the European Union, and urged the Prime Minister to take a tough line with the EU to get a better deal for the country.

Matthew gave me a sense of the business leaders who had already signed the letter. In the end, there were over 500. It was an impressive way to show momentum and that not all business leaders were wedded to the current terms of EU membership. It included one Stuart Rose, the former chair of iconic British brand M&S. Ironically, it was Rose who was later to be called up as the chair of the Remain campaign in 2016. Both camps were battling to win over iconic business leaders and British brands to their side.

Part of me thought it might be shrewd to sign on the line and keep the dialogue open with Business for Britain. With Cameron not yet having called a referendum, and with the Tories lacking a majority in Parliament, the plebiscite may never happen. What would I lose? I could get closer to the action of the Leavers and keep an eye on their activities for my clients. I believed that Brussels did need reform – I was never craven in my support for British EU membership – but I suppose I sensed the wider ambitions of the campaign. However, my heart and, most importantly, my head told me better; I was, after all, running the UK's largest City and financial sector lobbying agency, with a growing presence in Brussels. My corporates would not want to feed this endeavour. I guessed that they would not want me sleeping with the enemy.

It remains a real 'what if' moment for me. What if more corporates had signed that letter? Would there have been more influence on thinking and a chance to create better dialogue with the Leave campaign? Perhaps; perhaps not. But what was clear was that the Leave campaign had started in earnest with planning and energy, while on the Remain side of the equation there was nothing but squabbling about who might lead their efforts. The pro-EU politicians fought among themselves for months after the Bloomberg speech about leadership. And most of them – like myself – became embroiled in the 2014 Scottish independence question just at the time that the Leave campaign focused down on their main battle ahead. What was clear was that the pro-EU campaign would be miles behind the curve until Cameron and his No. 10 machine got a grip of their efforts (which turned out to be only after his negotiations with the EU were finalised in the early spring of 2016).

As we analysed the polls at the end of 2014, just a few months before the date set down for the 2015 election, it looked like Cameron was going to be back in power with Lib Dem help. For most of us lobbying for business, the political calculation was that, despite clamour in the Tory Party for that referendum, Nick Clegg and his Lib Dems would always block the move. Even if Ed Miliband ended up in No. 10 with the help of the SNP, the Labour Party were not putting Miliband under the same political pressure to offer a vote. No referendum, then!

But in December 2014 I sat down for breakfast with Liz Truss. We went to the Westminster favourite the Cinnamon Club (perhaps the poshest curry house in Britain, which does breakfast with a distinctly Indian twist). Newly appointed to the Cabinet as Cameron's Department for Environment, Food and Rural Affairs (DEFRA) Secretary of State, Liz had become a YouTube and *Have I Got News for You* sensation for her platform 'pork markets' speech to the Tory conference that year. In so many ways, that conference speech in 2014 has been the making of her. I offered Liz some wise counsel following that speech – I suggested she get her welly boots on and give BBC *Countryfile* a major interview in the weeks ahead. Sunday night prime time would be an opportunity for the nation to get to know her much better. She took my advice and appeared on the show in early 2015.

Over our breakfast eggs, I asked her how she was looking forward to another coalition with the Lib Dems. She smiled at me and confidently predicted: 'Iain – I think we are going to get a majority all on our own next year.' Really? Now, I had known Liz for years but, looking at the polls, I thought she was smoking something or had been spending too much time thinking about pork markets! Then, she told me something that I immediately relayed in anonymity in one of our client 'notes'.

> Iain – CCHQ [Tory Central Office] is sending me weekend
> after weekend down to the south-west. It's looking very, very
> good for us. I think there is going to be a Lib Dem wipeout
> round there. On the doorstep what we have promised on a
> whole number of issues and especially on the EU is cutting
> through with farmers and rural voters in particular.

Just five months later, Liz proved to be right. Her regular trips down to the south-west as DEFRA Secretary had worked, and she and the Tory machine had wiped Nick Clegg's party clean off the map for the first time in living memory. They were reduced to a tiny rump and replaced by the SNP as the UK's third force at Westminster.

The morning following the election result, I put into action plans to provide our clients with day-by-day notes updating them on the government's plans to hold that EU referendum. The idea that Cameron would be able to blame the Lib Dems for blocking the plebiscite had turned to dust. Business would need to start preparing in earnest for the campaign ahead.

But the consensus view was that the economics in favour of Yes would trump those of No to the EU. Of course, the entire framing of the question was something that would take business by surprise, when the UK Electoral Commission ruled out posing the question in such terms ahead of the campaign.

Some took my notes very seriously; others did not. Some of Britain's major businesses did start to plan for what might happen next, but the prevailing mood was clear: don't spend too much time or money on all this, there's no way Britain will vote to leave the EU.

But they weren't tuned in to what was happening. Matthew Elliott's grassroots work, which had begun almost two years earlier, was paying off. He had built a national operation without those EU-friendly corporates. He had also identified other 'self-made' business leaders, like James Dyson, who had seen the EU as an inhibitor to their growth and had built their empires in Asia, and Tim Martin, who had built his empire as a UK-only business regardless of the single market. Those names would resonate with voters more than those of the corporates. And by then the UKIP and Leave.EU work by Farage and Arron Banks was also in full swing, attracting a whole swathe of wider support.

In the summer of 2015, a Remain campaign was yet to grind into gear and get its act together to do any of this. Even at the party conference season of 2015, some business leaders who were pro-EU railed at Cameron for not getting behind the Remain campaign, which was at last forming. But Cameron thought he knew better. He still had his renegotiation to conclude and would not come out for Remain before then. It was all going to be fine in the end, wasn't it…

3

THE SCOTTISH PLAY

David Cameron liked referendums. He held three. Like Blair, his self-belief made him want to walk on political water. But in 2014, just two years before the EU referendum, business had a taste of that supreme self-confidence: the Scottish independence referendum, or IndyRef. The battle over whether Scotland would stay in or leave the UK would be decided with a simple Yes or No vote on a question put to the Scottish electorate: should Scotland be an independent country?

IndyRef shook the establishment, including commerce, to its core. The effect was amplified by the fact that, while Scotland may only make up around 8 per cent of the UK's entire population, it punches way above its weight in influence over the upper echelons of British national life and the deliberations therein. I'm happy to admit that as Scots we get a disproportionate say in the economic and political decisions our country takes – even David Cameron wanted to play up his Scottish ancestry as part of the 2014 campaign.

Cameron's predecessor as Prime Minister, Gordon Brown,

was a proud Scot, and Alistair Darling – another Scottish Labour Chancellor – held the tiller on the UK economy at its most momentous time in post-war history. The House of Commons is filled with Scots, and there are a large number among captains of industry and political, business and cultural commentators. Think Andrew Marr and Andrew Neil, who are some of the most authoritative opinion setters around. Some are political lobbyists too! You can count me in that club, though I'm equally happy to be called British and European as Scottish. So, there you have it – I've defined myself to you at the start of this chapter on the IndyRef campaign. That's identity politics right there – and it was identity politics that was to play a far larger part in the campaign in Scotland in 2014 than anyone would have predicted.

In so many ways, what happened in Scotland in 2014 was set to be a test drive for the EU referendum. In the summer of 2013, following the signing of the Edinburgh Agreement between Cameron and Salmond in October 2012, which unleashed the independence referendum, I tried to understand how businesses might fare in the campaign ahead. As a Scot, a Tory and a unionist, I also reached out to some figures across the political divide.

I had known Archy – now Lord – Kirkwood, the Liberal Democrat, for many years. When an MP for a seat in the Scottish Borders, he had chaired the Work and Pensions Select Committee for two parliaments in the early 2000s, and we had talked often about welfare reform. On 'saving the union', we knew we had a lot in common. He invited me to tea in Parliament to discuss what business might do in the campaign ahead. From fine House of Lords china I sipped my favoured peppermint tea while sat on the red benches of the tea room, which replicate those in the Lords chamber itself, and we both agreed that the nationalists already had momentum behind them, while the 'No' campaign had yet to fire up. This situation was to feel familiar in the summer of 2016. Concerned about customers and their political sympathies, business was silent; it felt trapped and unable to speak out.

Archy suggested we sit down with another notable Scottish politician. Days later, I was meeting Helen Liddell, former Labour Scottish Secretary under Blair, who had returned from a highly successful stint as High Commissioner in Australia and now sat in the Lords, like Archy. We had not met before – we came from very different political families – but Helen knew the threat that independence posed not just to the UK but, more narrowly, to the future fortunes of the Labour Party itself. Given Scotland had been sending busloads of Labour MPs to Westminster for the past fifty years, independence would likely kill off the chance of a future majority Labour government at Westminster. I outlined to both Helen and Archy how businesses might be able to support a No campaign but cautioned them both in those meetings: 'We need to ensure that Britain's bosses [based in London] are not being seen to tell Scots voters how to vote.' They were both in agreement and said that I needed to meet Alistair Darling to tell him the same.

After much soul-searching, Darling had been reluctantly brought into the debate to lead the fortunes of a cross-party No campaign. As he had been Chancellor, and given my work with the banking sector, I had worked with his team through the financial crisis, but we had not met in person through that period. And I was a Scots Tory! So I brought along someone from my own team at Cicero who was part of the Scottish Labour family to establish trust. Simon Fitzpatrick had joined my business in the early 2010s after working with Scottish Labour stalwart and former Treasury Select Committee chair John – now Lord – McFall.

With his Scottish Catholic roots – Simon's support for Celtic is an act of faith in every sense – he was steeped in the language of west of Scotland Labour politics, which was defined for many by its complicated attitude towards 'unionism'. Simon is a very canny operator. Undemonstrative, he nails insightful political analysis every time and decodes for the 'masters of finance' stuff they just don't know or even hope to understand for themselves. I remember him telling me that we should not use the word 'unionist' in the campaign or in the conversation with Alistair Darling. 'It will drive many Scots Labour votes in the west towards the SNP.' In my tradition, the Tory Party in Scotland has deliberately made association with the word 'unionist'.

We arrived at Darling's office in Portcullis House. Unlike Ken Clarke's room, it was a model of minimalism with virtually no papers or clutter. I remember catching sight of Tony Blair's autobiography rather ostentatiously displayed on the rather empty shelves. Of course, Darling and Brown had been firm allies until their time as Prime Minister and Chancellor together. Things were different by 2013 and Darling had written a brilliant page-turning autobiography of his own time as Chancellor, which – modestly – was not on display in his office the day we met. Brown and Darling had a tempestuous relationship as neighbours in Downing Street, as Darling had worked to ensure continued fiscal discipline in the midst of the unfolding global financial crisis, while Brown wanted to continue to spend.

We talked at length about how the campaign was taking time to put together and then how business might want to support it. 'How might they help?' asked Darling. I responded that there would be a wariness. Business knew that a large number of Scots – customers and employees – would back independence and they didn't want to antagonise them or lose business. But, when push came to shove, they would come out for the UK.

'The key thing is that the campaign must involve business in the strategy from the start,' I said, with Simon backing me up. 'Don't just ask them to "do stuff". They need time to make things work in their own way. They won't be dictated to last minute by the politicians.' However, despite Darling's best efforts, the No. 10 operation had other ideas when the campaign got up and running, with constant last-minute requests to come out for the 'union'. So often, it was those counterproductive and ill-timed requests that made pro-UK business feel they had been used for no benefit at all.

At the height of the campaign in the summer of 2014, my Cicero Group co-founder, Jeremy Swan (another Scot and a former Tory who had become a Lib Dem almost a decade earlier, subsequently working directly with Charles Kennedy and Nick Clegg), met with Deputy Prime Minister Clegg over a dinner hosted by Cicero and the Corporation of London in the Guildhall.

'The campaign is far too negative,' said Jeremy. 'It doesn't give any positive benefits about remaining in the UK.'

'I know – I know,' said Clegg, who, up close and personal, looked white as a sheet and increasingly drained by his experience in coalition with the Tories. 'But the polling and No. 10 are convinced it will work.'

Just like Matthew Elliott's operation, Business for Britain, pro-independence campaigners had created 'Business for Independence'. It was characterised by similar traits, mainly comprising SMEs, entrepreneurs and self-made businesses. Of course, 'big beasts' like the Souter family (who created the global Stagecoach bus empire) had also made big donations to the SNP at the time. It was designed to bring businesspeople into the Yes movement and be a grassroots recruiter for separation.

However, most larger businesses rejected independence; they preferred the union with the rest of the UK. Some had bankrolled the ailing Scots Tories for the long wilderness years. When feisty new Scottish Conservative leader Ruth Davidson launched herself on the scene in 2011, some of those corporate 'Tartan Tories' who had swapped voting for Maggie in the 1980s to being cheerleaders for a competent, efficient and business-friendly SNP administration began to think again. While they may have liked Salmond personally and admired his own political 'entrepreneurialism', they were fundamentally unionists at heart by inclination and upbringing.

When I spoke to boardrooms in Scotland and in London at the time, the most oft-repeated phrase to me was: 'I don't know anyone who is voting for independence. Who are these people?' My response to the captains of finance was usually: 'Well, you don't meet most people voting for independence when you are having a glass of the finest malt whisky in the Concorde lounge at Heathrow, do you?' Two worlds which never collided captured in a single sentence. The business elite's myopia during IndyRef was to be mirrored in 2016.

Nevertheless, there was one big name who backed independence, someone who was in charge of billions on global stock markets: Martin Gilbert, CEO of the EU's largest independent fund manager, then called Aberdeen Asset Management. I had known Martin for a large part of my life. Like me, he hails from Aberdeen, and we went to the same school, Robert Gordon's College (which is the same school Michael Gove attended). Martin and his wife Fiona have become family friends, and he is also one of my longest-standing clients.

We used to jibe with each other about independence – he knew my background in 'Toryland' – but we both wanted the best for Scotland. Given his deep business and personal economic interests across Scotland, but particularly across north-east Scotland, Martin had got to know Alex Salmond as First Minister very well. They regularly spoke and played golf together. In early September 2014, as the Scottish independence campaign reached its crescendo, Aberdeen Asset invited many of its key international investors and partners of the business (like myself) to attend the annual Braemar Gathering. Aberdeen Asset had held a biannual investor conference in Aberdeenshire to coincide with the Highland Games. It was to prove to be a dramatic weekend.

My husband and business partner Mark Twigg and I

joined a couple of hundred other people who had flown into the event from across the globe, attracted by some very warm hospitality and the star billing of Her Majesty the Queen, who was set to attend the most famous of all the Highland Games on the Saturday afternoon. In a hotel on the outskirts of Aberdeen on the afternoon of Friday 6 September 2014 – the day before the games, and just two weeks ahead of the independence poll – we were treated to Alex Salmond in conversation with Andrew Neil. As ever, Andrew Neil did not pull his punches, even in a private gathering with no TV cameras. Speaking for many present, he roasted Salmond on the issue of the currency and what Scotland would do if the UK government carried out its threat not to allow an independent Scotland to use the pound.

Major players like the then HSBC chair Douglas Flint were in the room with me to listen to the grilling. Douglas, like me, was on the other side of the argument from Salmond and had made it clear to the *Daily Telegraph* in a keynote commentary over the summer that he believed that Scotland should remain a part of the UK to secure its long-term prosperity.[12] But others took a different view. When speaking to me for this book, Martin Gilbert told me: 'I got involved with IndyRef because I think you either want to be a big country or a small one with a focus – an edge. That's why I backed Scottish independence.' Gilbert's intervention had created waves in Westminster, too, and I'm told many in Westminster, such as Chancellor George Osborne, were convinced his intervention might have swung it.

---

12 Douglas Flint, 'Scotland has to realise the pound has been a core part of its success', *Daily Telegraph*, 22 August 2014.

Salmond – always supremely confident – stayed for dinner that night with the mainly pro-union financiers following his afternoon cross-examination by Andrew Neil. He already sensed that a bombshell was about to hit the Braemar Gathering later that weekend. Momentum was moving to the case for independence. The SNP and other pro-separation campaigners had started their efforts way back in the early 2010s, with support for independence stuck at around a third of Scots voters for some time. By the time we heard Salmond speak on 6 September, the Yes campaign – chiefly powered by the SNP – was neck and neck with Better Together (the No campaign slogan, rebranded as 'No Thanks' near the end of the campaign).

The next day, a slight grogginess had taken effect among most of the gathered clan of finance folks. The malt whisky and the generous hospitality of the night before had kicked in on the bus ride up Royal Deeside to the Braemar gathering, but the group could not get away from the politics. Standing tall in fields on the riverside route were countless large US-style campaign posters erected by the farming community. The political geek within me started a pro- and anti-independence count. Across most of Scotland, pro-UK supporters had been somewhat wary of displaying their colours. Putting up posters was shunned by many anti-independence supporters. However, the countryside told a different story, with the vast majority of the posters on this journey backing Better Together. (Incidentally, Aberdeenshire – the county we were travelling through – ended up backing No by over 60 per cent.)

When the coaches carrying the global investors arrived at the historic Braemar Highland Games park, there were huge signs posted outside saying: 'No political campaigning inside the grounds.' Despite the large sign, however, the only topic of conversation over lunch was the politics all around us. Quite literally, we were surrounded by Union Jacks and Saltires, as well as the occasional campaign sticker rather self-consciously stuck onto the take-away food available around the grounds.

Salmond did not join the gathering. I had heard he had been asked to stay away from the event to ensure the Queen was not drawn into politics, but his former chief of staff Geoff Aberdein later told me: 'He was never due to be at the gathering. Protocol meant that he would not be there. In any case, there was campaigning to do.'

As the investors enjoyed lunch, talk flowed of money moving south from Scotland to London, 'just to be safe' – and there were numbers to prove it. According to Reuters: 'Investors pulled $27 billion (£16.6 billion) out of UK financial assets [in August 2014] – the biggest capital outflow since the Lehman crisis in 2008 – as concern mounted about the economic and financial consequences if Scotland left the UK.'[13]

By the time the gathering ended and the Queen had gone, we all travelled in convoy back to Aberdeen. My partner Mark and I were set to enjoy some of my parents' legendary hospitality on the Saturday night at our family home in Aberdeenshire. It was great to be back home with my parents. They have welcomed my other half into the family with open arms and being with them is one of the joys of my life. At the time, they lived in deepest Aberdeenshire, with a view

---

13 Jamie McGeever, 'Capital flows out of UK before Scots vote on independence, report shows', Reuters, 12 September 2014.

directly across to the Granite City. From the moment you walk into their house, you are enveloped with their love and kindness – and usually offered a fine drink to start proceedings. In the political madness of the past few years, they have always been a tremendous rock of stability for me in an ever-changing world.

As we tucked into mum's great cooking, my phone started to ping with messages from nervous clients who had spied Twitter. Salmond's glint in the eye on the Friday evening was for a reason. The *Sunday Times* was about to publish a YouGov poll showing a 1 per cent lead for the Yes campaign. I shuddered, and so did our entire family. Brought up in Scotland and proudly British, my family's sense of identity was under threat.

The next morning, the Sunday papers reflected on the poll, and later that day the BBC reported on a chance comment from the Queen outside Crathie Kirk at Balmoral, in which she said: 'I hope people will think very carefully about the future.' The Sovereign was worried about her sovereignty – and she was right to be.

We travelled back to London from Dyce Airport on the evening of 8 September with a sense of dread – accompanied by many of the financiers who had spent their weekend in Scotland with Martin Gilbert – and spent the entire week briefing domestic and international clients about the scenarios likely to play out. The Cicero client notes would be coming thick and fast now in the final two weeks of the campaign as most Westminster politicians cancelled politics as normal and raced to Scotland. But I continued to note that those who would take a big part in the forthcoming

EU referendum on the Leave side were nowhere to be seen. Many of them were focused on their prize and not the battle for Scotland. In fact, they often commented to me that they were tired of the debate on Scottish independence, which I decoded to mean that they regarded Scotland as likely to back No. They would be right about that.

By Monday 15 September, I was like a cat on a hot tin roof. I was due to be back in Scotland for 18 September 2014 – not to vote (I didn't get one as part of the wider non-resident diaspora) but to celebrate my father's eighty-second birthday. He and I had hoped it would not prove to be one of his last as a UK citizen.

I flew back to Aberdeen a day earlier than planned and spent 18 September at the Better Together phone bank in Aberdeen, calling voters. It was the most remarkable day of political campaigning that I had ever undertaken. Unlike most phone banking, where you have to coax and cajole, almost everyone I called had already voted very early that morning. Young and old, pro- and anti-independence, they had got up and gone to the polls after breakfast. In the end, the turnout was a record 85 per cent of the Scottish electorate.

Leaving the phone bank at around 7.30 p.m., I drove back to my parents' home in deepest Aberdeenshire. We were going to enjoy my father's birthday dinner regardless. On the way, I called an old friend, now also a fellow lobbyist, Rhoda MacDonald. From the Scottish Labour tradition, she had spent most of her day in Glasgow. 'I'm feeling really confident,' I said. 'Around Aberdeen and north-east Scotland, this feels like a big vote for No.' But through a cracking mobile line I could tell she was beyond anxious and almost in tears.

'Well, Glasgow feels really bad for No tonight. I reckon it has voted to leave,' she said. She would be proved right. 'Let's keep close tonight,' I replied, and headed home to a large glass of pinot noir to settle my nerves. While Aberdeenshire may have backed No, the huge numbers of voters in Scotland down in the central belt could easily tip the balance away from remaining in the UK.

After dinner, I sent out briefings to major clients – UK, Asian and US – to get them ahead of the politics. My phone lit up again. US markets started to show their jitters. By 11 p.m., the TV referendum results shows were in full swing, and I received a call from Sky News. They had spotted I was in Aberdeen sending cheery (if a little manic) pro-union tweets all day and talking up the positive turnout. They asked if I would be able to come down to Aberdeen Exhibition Centre around 2.30 a.m. to talk to Sky's Scotland correspondent, Niall Paterson. The producer told me that they had been expecting Salmond but had just heard that he was swithering about whether or not to turn up. They only expected him there for a triumphant appearance.

'Why not,' I said. 'I'm going to be up all night anyway.'

Around 2 a.m., I left my parents' house as quietly as possible and drove to the north-east Scotland count, where the Sky News channel crew had set up. Niall greeted me with a hearty handshake. 'Thank God you have turned up – Salmond's not coming now, and he's the only reason we came here in the first place.'

I gave Sky the latest reaction from international markets, who by then had worked out that Scotland was sticking with the UK. Asia was already trading sterling on that basis, and

investor sentiment was firmly up about the UK and its overall credit rating.

Scotland voted by 55 per cent to 45 per cent to stay. I went
home around 3.30 a.m. and bashed out a note to clients and
a blog for the Huffington Post. In an article titled 'The UK is
A-Changin', I began by saying: 'The only poll worth watching was the final one.' I continued: 'While commentators,
business and markets have twitched and twittered with the
gyrations of #indyref polls in the past month – NO has won
this referendum by a clear margin.'[14] Yet, despite being obviously delighted with the result, I added a word of caution
for those hoping for a quick reversion back to the status quo,
concluding: 'The Neverendum I think is off the table but all
of Britain will never be the same again after indyref.'

Despite there being a ten-point differential between Yes
and No in the referendum which was supposed to end the
debate 'for a generation', it did no such thing. Within hours,
Salmond had resigned as First Minister and within days as
SNP Deputy Leader, and Nicola Sturgeon, the overwhelming
favourite to serve as his successor, had given a keynote interview to *Newsnight* pointing to the likely impact of any future
EU referendum on Scottish politics. 'I think that is one of
the circumstances that would make many people in Scotland
think that it was time to think again,' she commented when
asked by Kirsty Wark what the impact of a UK-wide vote to
leave the EU would be, in the event that Scotland backed
Remain. Another Cicero client note went out, and we briefed
clients the following day. They shuddered once again.

---

14 Iain Anderson, 'The UK is A-Changin'', The Blog, HuffPost, 19 September 2014.

4

OH – THERE'S ANOTHER REFERENDUM COMING

I spent the first few months of 2015 dwelling on what Liz Truss had told me over breakfast – that Cameron was set to get a majority all of his own. It just didn't feel like that. The problem remained those darned opinion polls; the zeitgeist was that Ed Miliband was running Cameron close to the keys of No. 10.

Perhaps – like almost every other analyst – I should have kicked the pollsters harder on their models, which proved to be so way off beam. Perhaps I should have averted my eyes from the social media bubble of 'Milifandom' – the commentariat's confection of the times – which in the midst of that election campaign had the *Evening Standard* projecting Ed Miliband's head atop the torso of Aidan Turner's Poldark at the height of that Sunday night viewing pleasure for millions. It really was fantasy politics.

While the Labour leader had sharpened up his act for the general election, he was hampered by an aggressive and highly effective Tory advertising campaign which placed Miliband on a somewhat less aesthetic torso – and into Alex Salmond's top pocket. An election campaign that took place just eight months after IndyRef chimed with many voters. Cameron's words on the steps of Downing Street the morning after the Scottish referendum in 2014 calling for 'English votes for English laws' had resonated with millions south of the border who had begun to resent the share of government oxygen that Scotland had received over the previous two years. Beyond that, Liz Truss's campaigning skills in the south-west had clearly worked a treat. Cameron's coalition partners had been wiped out in one of their former heartlands, and a big driver of that newfound Tory support had been Cameron's pledge to hold an in/out EU referendum.

For business, what had seemed a remote prospect – the idea that Cameron would actually win power in his own right and then have to deliver on the plebiscite he promised way back in 2013 in his Bloomberg address – now became a reality. Within minutes of the chimes of Big Ben sounding at 10 p.m. on 7 May 2015, when the TV exit polls made clear that Cameron would increase the number of Conservative seats in the Commons against all expectations. As the night went on, it then became clear that he would have a working Conservative majority of his own, the text messages and emails from business leaders started arriving into my inbox. They all asked the same questions: 'When do you think the referendum will take place? What should we do? Should we take part in any campaign? Is there a chance that Cameron will back Leave? What will Labour do? Is there any chance that "Remain" [or "Yes", as many had thought that the question would be phrased] will lose?' I spent the night answering them in the following way.

Cameron would want to use the momentum of his unexpected victory to go for an early poll in 2016 after securing some kind of concession from Europe. He would place his personal political footprint all over this effort and the campaign would to a large extent be positioned in this way. It would be 'his' renegotiation and he would campaign for the public to back his approach. He believed – after securing his own majority in Parliament – that voters back him personally. If your business used the EU passport to access the single market, you would need to communicate its importance to policymakers on all sides of this debate. You also needed to communicate this early to those who work in your business, I warned – don't leave it until the last minute. Businesses telling people how to vote is never a good idea – look at what happened in the Scottish referendum – but if your brand has deep levels of trust, you should contribute to the debate. My view was that Cameron would firmly back Remain, but he had to do his renegotiation first. However, my fear was that he may have left the positive case for the EU far too late. The Labour leadership claimed to be totally pro-Remain – but I had doubts. On balance, I thought most people would vote Remain when the final vote came…

OK, so most of us got that wrong. But we did attempt to change the nature of the campaign to encourage them to do so. I also had to take a commercial view as well as making a political and personal judgement. Having worked with politicians like Ken Clarke, and having been pro-EU all my adult life, the decision might have appeared simple. In many ways it was. My professional career has brought me into contact with hundreds of businesses that actively used the EU supply chain and the passport. Many of those businesses had relocated to the UK from the US and Asia because of the ease of doing business across the EU inside the single market, as well as being drawn by the UK's positively pro-enterprise political culture for the previous thirty years. While I had many friends campaigning for the other side, my judgement was that the UK had barely climbed out of the effects of the financial crisis, and I was worn out too by the emotional impact on my identity of the Scottish independence poll. In fact, my own layered identity as Scottish, British and European all came to the fore in my mind. But, in the end, it was the economics for me that trumped the identity politics.

All our intelligence across the businesses we were already working with, as well as wider connections, provided robust and decisive. Over 90 per cent of them wanted to remain in the EU. We took a collective decision to make it clear that Cicero Group would support the Remain cause where possible. Beyond any personal viewpoint, it was simply good business to back Remain. However, as you will see later, we made sure to keep the channels open with Leave in order to monitor and track their activities and to be prepared for any outcome.

Within days, my diary was filling up with meetings from businesses starting to put together EU referendum strategy sessions. These typically involved the CEO and strategy directors, alongside the general counsel (chief legal officers), planning and regulatory teams, and the communications function. For most of these businesses, this had come as a bolt from the blue. They had not expected to need to do any of this. Frankly, while some took the job seriously, I felt others were just going through the motions to satisfy their regulator's or shareholders' questions in their quarterly results.

One of the most advanced in terms of thinking was Lloyds

of London – the centrepiece of the global reinsurance market, located in that iconic Richard Rogers structure in the heart of the City of London. Every time I go into the building, with its outside plumbing and gleaming futurist columns, I get a thrill. It's like walking into Parliament – albeit the building is a lot safer. History, commerce and a genuinely global perspective all lie within its walls. Its epicentre is the underwriting floor with the famous Lutine Bell, which is rung upon a shipping or natural disaster. It is an amazing sight. Its core purpose is to protect business and individuals from calamity and misfortune, and to allow enterprises to scale up despite the myriad economic, climatic and geopolitical threats we face. Perhaps it was no surprise that Lloyds appeared to be my best-preparing client!

But leadership is key in any business and the then Lloyds CEO Inga Beale and her then general counsel Sean McGovern struck me as some of the most far-sighted business leaders of the time. They both knew that Brexit would pose a significant challenge to the current Lloyds of London business model and they wanted to keep an active track on the likely politics ahead, as well as creating a working series of scenario plans to allow the London market to adapt quickly in the event of a vote to leave the EU. Speaking to me in early 2019, Beale said: 'We had to be ready. Many businesses left preparations until after the result of the referendum. We felt we simply didn't have that choice. We wanted to get ahead of the game.'

What did they want me and my team to do? Initially, a planning group started small and met on a monthly basis. My team would provide the latest polling data on the in/out (Remain versus Leave) question, alongside political risk intelligence from Westminster and Brussels on the likely timing of Cameron EU's renegotiation and the timing of the poll itself. Given my earlier interactions with Business for Britain and Matthew Elliott's work, we also needed to keep an eye on the developing business campaign groups in favour of Leave. Around the table with us also were the legal and planning teams who were starting to look deeply at the interconnected passporting arrangements and aiming to seek out a solution in case the UK was to leave the single market. I remember the most oft-repeated phrase in those early meetings in the summer of 2015 was: 'Surely Cameron will want to get this referendum over and done with before there is another summer of awful news from the migrant crisis.' Many of the global businesses that invested in the UK had seen the impact that the migrant crisis was having on France and Italy, and Germany in particular.

Let me explain some more about how I had pieced this together. Over the past decade I have spent more time with politicians from Angela Merkel's party – the Christian Democratic Union (CDU) – than virtually any other group in the EU. It made sense: German politicians had an outsized influence on EU decision making. David Cameron had sensechecked his Bloomberg speech meticulously with Merkel back in 2013 by means of a heck of a lot of shuttle diplomacy by his Europe minister, David Lidington. Every autumn since 2012 I have travelled to the shores of Lake Como in Italy to spend time with the Konrad Adenauer Foundation (KAS) at Adenauer's former lakeside holiday home in Cadenabbia. It is a beautiful place in the northern Italian lakes; its grand house on a hill, where Adenauer used to take time away from the affairs of state, is complemented by a very comfortable conference centre, with a dormitory for the delegates. The views from the house across the lake are exceptional, and it is fair to say you are fed well with Italian pastas and wines.

Adenauer was the first Chancellor of the post-war Federal Republic. KAS is an international ambassadorial outreach arm of the CDU – the party that the Tories used to caucus alongside in the European People's Party grouping in the European Parliament before Cameron yanked his party out of it in 2009. KAS still brings together UK Conservative MPs and MEPs, CDU MEPs and Bundestag members alongside commentators and businesspeople. For me, it has been a vital way for us to understand each other's viewpoints over the past decade as the UK's dislocation from the EU has grown, and it has been an essential back channel for the Tory and CDU politicians no longer caucusing together in the EU. One of those crucial conversations for me has been listening in to the positivity of the CDU politicians opening their arms to the migrant crisis in the mid-2010s then turning towards their real concerns that this had fed the rise of Alternative for Germany (AfD), the country's most Eurosceptic party. The debate on immigration which had inflamed the debate on EU membership in the UK was now taking place in Germany, but it was instructive to watch how very different conclusions were drawn by Germany's major centre-right party on the question of continued EU membership. They viewed EU solidarity as the way to solve the problem. Just as we have seen with the Cameron veto of the amendment to the Lisbon Treaty, the UK centre-right party took a very different approach.

The KAS meetings were, and remain, an opportunity for

German policymakers to understand UK political and business activities and to talk frankly, freely and privately. Never once did I hear before or after the referendum that a major German business would intervene with German politicians to say: 'We need the UK market so let's cut a great deal with Britain.' It was a fundamental misreading of the psychology of German business leaders by UK politicians to ever expect that – a misreading that built up as a result of a lack of real dialogue between the two. While I have argued earlier that David Cameron's decision to leave the EPP was a significant error, in so many ways it has created an opportunity for lobbyists like me. With the Tories cut off from their former partners, the intelligence gained from keeping the door open and listening directly to political and business leaders in Germany and France in particular is rare and valuable. It is insight that business needs to know and understand.

It was this kind of intelligence I aimed to bring back to businesses in the UK, like Lloyds of London, who were trying to figure out what was going on. Further, understanding how the actions of British business will play with EU politicians has become so important to understand and decode as a result of the EU referendum. In the years ahead, this decoding is going to be even more important than ever for both UK and EU-led business.

Let me briefly come back to the UK domestic scene before telling my story of the Brexit campaign. Another dramatic and unforeseen impact on business emerged in the summer of 2015, which was ultimately to have a real impact on the referendum outcome: the election of Jeremy Corbyn, the most left-leaning Labour leader in modern times. Just as businesses were asking me to unpack Brexit, suddenly they also wanted to understand what a hard-left Labour leader would want to achieve. I remember attending the 2015 Labour conference as a lobbyist – for the first time in living memory I was not very welcome, and the newly elected Labour leadership in those early days liked it that way. Twelve years after the 2003 Tory conference that had seen relations between the Tories and business at their lowest ebb, business just seemed nonplussed by Labour. But in the late summer of 2015, the idea of Jeremy Corbyn ever entering Downing Street as Prime Minister looked to be as unrealistic as Britain leaving the EU for most businesses, not to mention the pundits.

Before Cameron had completed his renegotiation with the EU, the two camps in the referendum ahead had started to form, and Leave was getting much more airtime, with some eye-catching pranks that TV news programmes loved. On 9 November 2015, Leave campaigners had disrupted the usually sedate CBI annual conference. They heckled the Prime Minister's speech, chanting that the CBI was the 'voice of Brussels'. Trying to get the cameras to turn back to him, an initially unnerved Cameron said: 'Come on, guys, you can ask me a question rather than making a fool of yourselves by just standing up and protesting.' While the protestors were quickly removed, they later told Reuters that they had disrupted the conference proceedings on behalf of Vote Leave – which was to become the designated Leave campaign in April 2016.[15]

The CBI delegates didn't know what had hit them, but they

---

15 David Milliken and Kylie MacLellan, 'Ireland says facing major strategic risk from Brexit', Reuters, 9 November 2015.

found Cameron, as always, to be reassuring. After a moment or two of moving about uncomfortably in their seats, they quickly regained their poise, mostly unaware that the seven months ahead would make for a very unsettling ride. The next day, Cameron was due to write to Jean-Claude Juncker to start the renegotiation of Britain's place in the EU.

Around the same time, I attended the launch of the Stronger In campaign in an old factory in east London. The venue was packed with business types, lobby groups and some of my own clients. But even before the event began, I noticed that something didn't feel right. The event didn't capture the political mood in 2015 – it felt more like a New Labour rally back in 1997 or 2001, at the height of the love-in between business and Blair. All optics and not a lot of substance. I can only say that the launch was an utter disaster in every way possible. It missed what had been happening in Britain over the previous few years. It looked flat and uninspiring. The business-heavy audience shuffled nervously in their seats. They had spent years recruiting former political campaigners like me to advise their businesses, but this launch looked distinctly past its sell-by date.

The brilliant retailer Stuart Rose, the former Marks & Spencer CEO, had been pushed front and centre to lead the campaign despite his own protestations that he was not a politician and had – as mentioned earlier – been an early tentative backer of the Eurosceptic Business for Britain. Rose later appeared in front of the Treasury Select Committee in early 2016 as chair of the campaign and gave the Vote Leave campaign one of their earliest, best and most oft-repeated soundbites when he commented, on a possible increase in wages if free movement was to come to an end: 'Yes, but that is not necessarily a good thing.'

At the end of the launch event, I sat quietly at the back of the room. I watched as serious business leaders melted away, nonplussed and clearly worried that the campaign was in bad shape from the get-go. BBC political editor Laura Kuenssberg came to sit down and join me. Laura and I had got to know each other over the past few years, especially when she took the shrewd move to switch from the BBC, where she had been the chief political correspondent, to ITV News, where she became business editor. In her ITV role, we spoke from time to time as she deepened her understanding of business. Most importantly, she had gained the badge of editor and got to know the world of commerce just at the right time in advance of the EU referendum. She knew who to call and how to gauge their opinions. By the time she came back to the BBC as its new political editor, her address book was filled with business as well as political contacts.

'How do you think that went?' she asked me. 'A bloody disaster,' was my response. Then we sat equally bewildered as top City spinner and Remain campaign grandee Roland Rudd invited what appeared to be his family onto the stage, where they all sat on the set while the tabloid snappers took photographs of them like the royal family posing for a rather relaxed wedding portrait. Laura and I looked at each other in disbelief. What was really going on here? It was a strange sight, and one which I have found impossible to erase from my memory to this day.

By the time the Cameron renegotiation had been completed in early March, business was on tenterhooks and hungry for any sliver of information about the final deal with the EU and how the Cabinet would react. We already knew that collective responsibility would be suspended for the campaign, and that ministers like Chris Grayling were itching to start making the argument for Leave, but when senior Tories Michael Gove and Boris Johnson dramatically came out for Leave, most businesses started to adjust their comfortable calculations that Remain would easily win. Business knew and liked them both in the earlier part of the decade; Boris in particular had spent a lot of time courting business as Mayor of London. It was in that period, when a total of five members of Cameron's Cabinet backed the 'other side', that most businesses started to significantly up the weight of their planning and preparation for the potential of Brexit, in the knowledge that both Gove and Johnson had the potential to sway the country. Nonetheless, there was still a widespread belief that sense would prevail and Leave would lose based purely on the economic forecasts.

Following the Cameron renegotiation, Anand Menon, director of The UK in a Changing Europe, was dismissive about the overall impact of the deal on the outcome of the referendum, in an article published on 24 February 2016.

What was striking in this first weekend of the campaign itself was how quickly the deal seems to have been forgotten. From an obsession with the terms of the deal on Saturday, the British media has moved quickly and seamlessly to a consideration of who will be on which side, and what the 'big issues' are.[16]

---

16 Anand Menon, 'David Cameron's renegotiation has failed to win Tory MPs around', *Daily Telegraph*, 24 February 2016.

In fact, back in August 2015 I had written my regular political column for *Square Mile*, the glossy magazine which is akin to *GQ* for those working in the City of London. Amid its pages of superyachts and supermodels, it has provided me with an outlet to range across our politics for the past few years. My words would prove to be strangely prophetic:

> The Prime Minister will look to spin his renegotiation as a historic success. So, difficult to do but it might include the UK opting out of 'ever closer union', benefit restrictions, recognition of a multi-currency EU and perhaps a red-card system for new EU legislation that allows national parliaments the ability to block new EU laws.[17]

In February 2016, the British Chambers of Commerce found that nearly two-thirds (63 per cent) of the 2,000 senior businesspeople surveyed stated that the renegotiation deal was unlikely to change how they would vote in an EU referendum. The BCC found that 59.5 per cent of those surveyed were intending to vote for the UK to stay in the EU, while 30.1 per cent were planning on voting to leave.

In order to better inform the businesses we worked with, I invited the directors of both official campaigns to come and talk to an audience at Cicero Group. We regularly host 'in conversation' events to broaden our thinking and encourage clients to have an open dialogue with key political protagonists. In terms of the modus operandi of the events, think *Newsnight*'s interview format with a heavy emphasis on the

---

17 'Iain Anderson on the EU Neverendum', *Square Mile*, 26 August 2015.

economics and business agenda. The audience is a mix of in-house lobbyists themselves, usually people from a political or policy background who have a deep understanding of the use of political language and the signals being sent, and senior businesspeople who work at boardroom level. Both Matthew Elliott from Vote Leave and Will Straw from Stronger In accepted my invitation to speak at different events. I knew Matthew better than Will as a result of my own politics, but I invited our director of UK public affairs (that's another term for lobbying), Tom Frackowiak, to interview them both. Our auditorium was packed out for both events and there is no doubt the sympathies in the room were with Straw.

However, the reaction from clients – many of whom came to both events – was clear. While most of them agreed with Straw, objectively they thought that Matthew had delivered a more compelling and emotionally convincing case. That was surprising because most of the business in the room had come from services sectors, which comprise almost 80 per cent of the UK economy, and Matthew had not been able to directly answer questions about what leaving might mean for services access to the single market. We would have to wait until the end of 2016 – after the referendum itself – for a plan to emerge for services around a form of 'enhanced equivalence' – that is, a comprehensive mechanism to allow the UK and the EU27 to recognise each other's rules and legislative framework – on which I write later in this book. But business left the room even more convinced that Vote Leave were pulling on strings with the electorate that just might work.

The events with Elliott and Straw both took place just

before 'purdah', the pre-referendum period during which the government machine is disabled and only the politicians and the campaigners are able to make the case in their designated campaigns. Civil servants would have to sit out the campaign, as they do during elections. Around that time, I invited Douglas Flint to come and make a keynote speech at Cicero. I knew Douglas and had worked with him for some time around TheCityUK table. TheCityUK was the body set up by former Chancellor Alistair Darling following the financial crisis in the late 2000s and which was given ongoing momentum when George Osborne came to the Treasury in order to represent the financial and professional services sector to policymakers and voters at home and abroad. My team had been in on the creation of the narrative for TheCityUK since its launch.

Douglas and I agreed on most things, from being opposed to Scottish independence to being concerned that leaving the EU would cause great upheaval to our economy and to the financial sector, which was only just recovering from the crash of 2007–09. Flint spoke just as purdah kicked in, and he made the case that the economic argument had already been won by the Remain campaign but that the wider societal debate was yet to be had in the country now that the government was disabled for the period ahead. He correctly opined that it would be the combination of economic *and* societal arguments that would hold sway with the electorate in the final weeks. He was and remains one of the few businesspeople to understand the wider societal impact arguments: that business does not operate in a vacuum and only obtains its legitimacy from the communities in which it operates. I often think that if more businesses had made and understood that case, things would be different now.

Around the same time, I was campaigning – outside of work – for Remain and was sent to speak at various events across the UK. The script I was sent from Stronger In – by now the designated Remain campaign – was really useless. Dry macro-management speak, it built no wider societal or emotional connection. I kept asking myself, who is writing this stuff? But it was clear when I went to speak at events well outside the London bubble or on its cusp that the debate taking place in the rest of the country was very different. One night I travelled to Chipping Barnet in north London to speak for Stronger In at a debate organised by the local Conservative association. I arrived to be greeted by the chair of the event, who told me that she would be supporting Leave but would try not to show her colours in the debate. But, in the end, she couldn't help herself when we got going, and interrupted me constantly. There was obviously a speaker from Vote Leave, which was fine, but then up popped another person on the platform, who had been asked to write a paper on the arguments for the local association and who then declared for Leave. Basically, I was one against three on the panel. I invoked the Scottish referendum only two years earlier to try to persuade moderates in the room to vote Remain to ensure we kept the UK together. There was not a flicker in response to my arguments. Everyone was very polite, but minds appeared closed.

I took those debates back to the day job to inform business that, despite the opinion polls, the result was set to be very close indeed. On the ground, things were very difficult from the highfalutin Cameron campaign. More and more businesses started to plan for a Leave outcome, while remaining bemused that this could be possible. Of course, business hates the idea of 'sunk costs' – that is, deadweight costs which an enterprise has to spend with no guarantee that the spending will actually be needed – so many businesses continued to plan ahead with the bare minimum resources in order to avoid costs which were still – it was thought – likely to be wasted when the UK voted to remain in the EU.

At the same time, business was coming under huge pressure to come out for Remain or Leave, but most were scarred by the experience of the Scottish referendum. Speaking to me for this book, David Cameron's communications director in Downing Street, Craig Oliver, told me: 'It was hard to get business to speak up – they feared a backlash. George Osborne used to say to me, "Don't count on business to do anything – we'll have to do it all ourselves."'

Oliver also reflected on the way in which businesses would want to speak in the political arena:

They just don't get it. When business speaks, it does so in a very corporate way. The words have been sieved through endless layers of corporate communications bullshit. Businesses need to do 'pub talk' – like Farage does – and speak about how they love their communities and how they give people a chance in life.

Former CBI president Paul Drechsler told me: 'I found myself begging – literally begging – some CEOs to speak up. But many had been burnt by the experience of the Scottish independence referendum. Some just told me, "That's why we pay you – to speak up for us."'

Of course the bigger problem was that many people felt uncomfortable with telling people how to vote. Drechsler said: 'This was not about telling people how to vote – it was about laying out what it meant for business so that people could make their own minds up. Overall, I agree with Osborne – there was a failure of enough businesses to speak out.'

On referendum day itself, I spent the afternoon campaigning in Wimbledon, where I live, handing out leaflets outside the station. By the end of the day it was clear to me that over 70 per cent of voters there had backed Remain. (My political nose was right, as the Wimbledon constituency voted 70.63 per cent to remain.) But during the day I called friends and colleagues campaigning outside London. Their mood was very different. There were echoes of my experience in Scotland two years earlier. They were expecting a majority Leave vote. I communicated this intelligence back to clients in the UK and across Europe, the US and Asia before the polls had even closed. It's fair to say that no one really believed it.

Around 8 p.m., I got home, showered and changed and took a very urbanite Uber to the Royal Festival Hall to the Remain 'victory' party. With its magnificent views across the Thames and London from the top of the building, it remains an iconic venue. The TV crews were there in earnest, and my Cicero Group colleague and former Sky News producer Kate McAndrew introduced me to Sky's Kay Burley. We agreed to do an interview on the reaction of business later in the evening when more of the results had emerged. Kate and I grabbed a drink and watched the early results while I kept an eye on the markets and the value of the pound on my smartphone.

Almost twenty years earlier, New Labour had gathered on the South Bank to celebrate Blair's victory. As a Tory, I had felt that the Stronger In launch had reeked of Blairism. There was something making me uneasy about the night of 23 June 2016, too. As I grabbed a beer, I couldn't quite make sense of it all. As usual, the pound was being monitored by currency traders all night, but, unusually, it was also being traded all night out of London itself. Despite the early concessions from Nigel Farage, who had accepted defeat before a vote was even counted that night, something continued to make me feel very nervous.

I spotted Gabe Winn, the Stronger In campaign's director of business engagement and a former FTSE 100 communications chief himself, and grabbed another drink with him, and then bumped into former Trades Union Congress general secretary Brendan Barber with his daughter Sarah, whom I have got to know through her work for one of Cicero's clients. Both looked confident. But, minutes later, Paddy Ashdown came rushing into the party. He needed a drink. He had got wind of early postal voting results, which were showing a big lead for Leave. It seemed the Vote Leave operation had timed their campaigning to perfection by maximising the message on immigration, not only in time for purdah but also when postal ballots would be landing on doorsteps. Vote Leave strategist Dominic Cummings had been winning the data wars and knew exactly what messages to push to whom and when.

Moments later, at around 11.30 p.m., I spied Craig Oliver. We had been friends since university and had grown up in Aberdeenshire. 'Feeling confident, Craig?' I asked. 'I just don't know,' he replied. I followed up with: 'Is the big man coming to the party?' 'No,' was his short answer, before he quickly headed back to No. 10 after barely half an hour at the party. I got the impression Oliver had seen the early postal voting returns too. Around the same time, Liz Truss wafted into the party; within minutes she had left. Liz – as I have indicated before – has a very keen political antenna.

By 1 a.m., when the result from Sunderland was announced with a 61 per cent vote to leave – despite a major intervention from Nissan warning about the supply-chain issues which Brexit might cause – I ordered another Uber. What was about to unfold was clear to me. Leave had the momentum to win. Accompanied by Kate McAndrew, I asked the cab to take me to my office in the City. As we travelled down Fleet Street, we reckoned that the City would be waking up much earlier than usual on 24 June 2016. And so it was to be. By 3 a.m., when the result of the referendum was beyond doubt, there started to appear an hourly batch of taxis taking bankers and City traders into their offices. The Japanese bank opposite my office had been almost empty at 3 a.m. save one or two staff keeping an eye on the referendum. By 5 a.m. I saw the desks on every floor had filled up; it looked like a normal working day.

I stood watching as the world changed in front of me, with my business partners Jeremy Swan and Mark Twigg alongside me. Like many other companies, we thought it was time to put in place a new and very different business plan.

5

GRIEF REIGNS IN BUSINESS

Friday 24 June 2016 was to prove the longest day. Having been up all night decoding the political earthquake of Brexit, my colleagues organised a conference call with our key clients to bring them up to speed with the consequences of what Britain had just done. Client notes were unable to keep up with the unfolding events around us. Our director of public affairs Tom Frackowiak gathered a team in our boardroom around 8 a.m. Events continued to move apace and we had been told to expect a statement from David Cameron on the steps of Downing Street during our client briefing. The enormous television in our meeting room had been switched on all night – we kept it on while we began the meeting.

Over 500 people had dialled into the Cicero call from far and wide. In fact, there were more people online from outside the UK, with clients up and about on Wall Street at 3 a.m., as well as some rather anxious markets types in Asia, who had been trading in earnest since they got to their desks at midnight UK time, just as the earliest results had started to emerge. People on the call were punch drunk. Many of them had, like me, been up all night. Most of them had got up early

– around 5 a.m., just as the final results had been trickling through – and they could not believe their ears.

In these conference calls it is our job to project beyond the immediate headlines that businesses can read in the newspapers or watch on the TV news, towards the politics and decisions ahead. But that morning, with my voice creaking from lack of sleep and nervous energy, I felt as if I had turned into a sporting commentator. Just as we started our call with clients, David Cameron walked out on the steps of Downing Street and announced two things.

The most important thing, for everyone watching, was that he intended to resign and initiate a Tory leadership contest almost immediately. Having seen Craig Oliver's demeanour only eight hours earlier at what was to prove to be the Stronger In wake at the Royal Festival Hall, I was not surprised. But the fact that this most business-friendly of Prime Ministers was about to walk off the stage made me say to clients that it was highly likely the next occupant of No. 10 was not going to be so inclined towards the corporate sector, given its support for the losing side. Weeks later, when he was briefly a backbench MP, I received a personal note from Cameron thanking me for signing the endless business letters arguing for Remain which had appeared in the national newspapers, which had been one of the tactics of the Cameron government and the Remain effort. However, it had proved to be a diminishing asset. Everyone in business – whichever side they had supported – sensed that things would now be rather different.

Most corporate business had been on the 'wrong' side of the campaign. Was it about to pay a political and economic price? Who would be the new Prime Minister? Would the corporate sector be shut out of Downing Street? Would fiscal and regulatory policy be tightened? Those questions were uppermost in business leaders' minds that morning, along-side what would now happen with the relationship with the EU. Would single market access be obtainable? What would happen to labour markets and immigration policy? Was there a chance that the UK might think again? But my over-riding memory from that morning after the night before was the sense of the business world – normally so articulate and composed – being all at sea, unable to find the words, ex-hausted by the politics and unable to work out its next steps. This feeling was to last for months ahead.

The other announcement that David Cameron made on the steps of Downing Street was to prove perhaps even more significant. He announced his 'Two Olivers' strategy. He had asked Oliver Letwin – the Tory Cabinet Office minister who had been embedded in Conservative policy thinking since the days of Margaret Thatcher – to become the Prime Min-ister's chief European adviser. This was a post that Letwin would occupy for around three weeks. Alongside him sat a career civil servant, Olly Robbins. Both were later to play key roles in the development of the entire Brexit saga. Before the Department for Exiting the European Union (inele-gantly referred to as DExEU) was created by Theresa May, the two Ollies got to work in the Cabinet Office with three initial aims: firstly, to reach out to the EU to put in place the dialogues that would be needed to start the negotiations; secondly, to reach out across the House of Commons to at-tempt to establish a political consensus; and, finally, to reach out to those beyond politics, including business, to attempt to achieve a national consensus. But, by 14 July, Letwin was gone and the strategy of consensus and reaching out had been ripped up.

Speaking to Nick Robinson's Political Thinking BBC podcast in spring 2019, Letwin admitted: 'We were all on the way out, but I was trying to prepare the ground. It became rapidly apparent to me that the sensible thing to do was to try and get a complete cross-party agreement as Varadkar did with his counterparts in the Dáil.'

It would not take long before business realised it was going to be firmly locked out of any input to the decision making.

I had felt very disoriented by the result. I had to hibernate for the weekend after the referendum and just sleep. I think that's what those who have lost campaigns usually do as the adrenalin seeps out of you. For the winning side, a new, fresh surge of adrenalin kicks in. But despite my attempts at rest, the calls from clients would not go away. I had never seen business leaders respond with such emotion. Business is supposed to be a rational act – successful business, certainly. It is governed by making cool-headed judgements and carrying them out with care and diligence. None of those behaviours were on display in the early days and weeks after the referendum. For some, there was a sense of panic; for most, I witnessed an initial numbness, and from a few there was real anger.

As my London team was briefing clients on the morning after the referendum, my Brussels office was having to go into bat on behalf of our clients at the centre of the EU. Cicero's Brussels director, Helena Walsh, is steeped in the culture and the nuance of the EU scene, having worked in the European Parliament and for the Irish inward investment agency there. She emailed me after having taken one of our UK clients into the Commission just hours after the UK had voted to leave. 'It was like the elephant in the room,' she said. 'You just couldn't talk about it.' She later reflected to me that for UK businesses coming to talk to EU policymakers in that heady initial summer, the conversation had changed. There was a chill in the air and MEPs wanted to know a lot more about the operations and economic activity taking place inside the EU and in the home states than that which was taking place in the UK itself.

Back in the UK, a Conservative leadership election needed to be navigated for business. With Boris, Gove, Leadsom and Fox all on the Leave side, there was not a lot of choice for those who had backed Remain and wanted to see the softest Brexit landing possible, one that might hold out the prospect of single market or at least customs union membership. Theresa May had been on the Remain side. Just.

Within days, I was speaking to Katie Perrior, who was to become Theresa May's chief spokesperson in Downing Street in her first year until the 2017 election campaign. I offered to help with business support. I also spoke to Robert Buckland MP, the solicitor general, who had been garnering campaign support and was on board with Theresa. As I reached out to businesses for help, I was met with a positive response – so positive that the news that I was helping was bound to leak. And so it did – I took a call from *PRWeek*, who wanted to talk about me 'getting involved with the campaign'. I was happy to confirm this, as I thought it would be a way for business support to find its way towards the effort. However, within minutes of the story appearing, I received a text from Buckland. 'You need to calm this down,' he said. 'Fiona is going berserk.' He was referring to Fiona Hill, one of the Prime Minister's joint chiefs of staff. I subsequently learned that the real concern was about business being seen to get too close to the May leadership campaign – and a lobbyist being involved at all. Given that Fiona had briefly also been a lobbyist for business, I thought this more than a little surprising, but it proved to be a useful insight for what was to lie ahead in the May administration's attitude to business.

I often think that perhaps I should have done something much more counter-intuitive and supported someone who really did back Leave, someone like my old school friend Michael Gove. Speaking to Treasury Select Committee chair Nicky Morgan MP for this book, I asked her why she had backed Michael, given her own prominent role as a Remainer in 2016. She told me: 'Because it had to be a Brexiteer to take over the leadership in 2016. It had to be someone who was able to say, "Look guys, you know I'm a Leaver, but here are the compromises we have to make in order to get ourselves out of the EU."' Of course, Morgan backed Gove a second time in the next Conservative leadership battle, in the summer of 2019.

As the other candidates fell away, and Andrea Leadsom withdrew from the leadership campaign for reasons which are well documented elsewhere, Theresa May was the last woman standing. As she spoke in Birmingham to launch her manifesto, there was a heavy tilt in her words towards changing the deal between business and the electorate. She launched the idea of 'workers on boards' – a policy idea to have employee representatives on major company boards, which had echoes of a similar approach taken in Germany. It was a neat counterpoint to Corbyn economics and one which might resonate. I could now see why Fiona Hill wanted to keep business out of the May campaign.

On 13 July 2016, Theresa May walked into Downing Street as Prime Minister and talked about bringing the country together again – as well as the 'burning injustices' she wanted to solve in British society. (Throughout her time in No. 10, you could read that speech in the Downing Street waiting room, just off the main entrance hall. Every time I did, I thought of the resonance of those words and the opportunity which had been lost.) But that day, as I watched the Prime Minister live, my mind wandered back to 2007, when Gordon Brown had walked into Downing Street. Similar political notes had been chimed: two leaders who would face an existential crisis under their leadership. The only difference being that May knew what she was taking on when she entered office. Brown really did not.

I, meanwhile, had flown out of Britain for the day. There was real business to do. In the immediate aftermath of the result, business had asked me to start to look at location options inside the EU to take advantage of the single market passport needs. Without any guarantees from the government and the EU, business was sizing up its options for the future to secure the access it needed to its largest market. I also had another thought in mind: how would Cicero adapt and grow through this environment? Like many other businesses, we had sat down as a board to work out the range of options available to us to both protect and grow our market following the referendum. Given that a large amount of our business was with financial markets – banks, insurers, investors, infrastructure players, tech players and asset managers – there were only one or two location options that would be attractive.

Thus, Helena Walsh and I got on a plane to Dublin. As both our lead director in Brussels and an Irish citizen, Helena's deep understanding of Ireland would serve us well. We had a day of meetings to test the appetite of the Irish authorities and relay this intelligence back to clients who had been using the UK as their primary passport location back into the EU up until now.

Our first meeting was with officials from the Irish Ministry of Finance. On walking away from that initial encounter, Helena and I had the overriding view that Ireland did not want to see a headlong rush of businesses arriving at their door. Our next meeting was with the Central Bank of Ireland, the chief regulator for the financial sector, and it only added to that view. 'We don't want to see any brass-plating operating models,' said a senior official. 'We have been through that before. We want to see substance locating here.' ('Substance' was code for jobs, and lots of them.) Brass-plating is a reference to the operating model used before the financial crisis back in 2008. A lot of financial business had opened in Dublin in the 1990s and 2000s, but there had not been huge numbers of jobs created in the city as a result – a fact that had annoyed many Irish politicians. So, while the Irish exchequer gained the tax from corporate entities which had set up in Dublin, they didn't gain any wider societal benefits. More than that, when the financial crisis took hold in 2008–09, Ireland found itself sitting atop a financial debt mountain that dwarfed the Irish economy. Irish policymakers were not going to make the same mistake again.

Later that day we met with Fianna Fáil, the main Irish opposition party. It was clear they believed that Fine Gael, the lead partner in the confidence and supply deal, was not taking advantage of the Brexit 'dividend', as they saw it. That cautiousness maintained itself for the rest of the summer, but the Irish government had moved into a much more upfront marketing mode. So much so that I hosted Ireland's then Finance Minister Eóghan Murphy at Cicero in London, in front of a packed audience. He had a smile already on his face, as he was taking back to Ireland commitments from some of the major investment banks, like Citi and Barclays, to boost their presence in the country. I also noted Murphy as one of the most adept EU politicians I had encountered anywhere and one I still regard as a future Taoiseach.

However, while Ireland set out a tough line on 'substance' and 'brass-plating', other EU centres such as Frankfurt, Amsterdam, Berlin and Paris took a very different approach. In fact, in the weeks following the Brexit vote, Berlin started a very vocal advertising campaign in the City of London, sending advertising vans around the UK's financial centre, to the bemusement of onlookers. France, meanwhile, rolled out the red carpet of its diplomatic machine, hosting senior business leaders at its London Embassy and uncorking the finest burgundies and clarets.

As Helena and I travelled back to Dublin Airport just in time to watch Theresa May enter Downing Street as Prime

Minister, we reflected on our day of meetings. Our message to clients would be that Ireland will welcome you only if you are bringing jobs and tax – in substantial amounts. We also resolved to create a business plan to launch an Irish operation ourselves when we had enough client substance to do so. This was to be our own Brexit 'hedge', to allow us to serve clients who were likely to want to lobby inside the EU. We opened Cicero Ireland in February 2018.

After my trip to Dublin, and watching Boris Johnson, David Davis and Liam Fox settle into their new Cabinet chairs, I needed to have a break. We had long planned to take a road trip from San Diego to Seattle in late July 2016. It was a brilliant holiday and we fell in love with north California, earmarking it as a potential home one day. (I have been back since to enjoy the pinot noirs.) The fact that we were also eight hours behind the UK working day meant I left British politics and Brexit far behind. Of course, along our journey I could not get away from the raging battle between Donald Trump and Hillary Clinton to become the forty-fifth President of the United States. From the 'build a wall' posters by the border in San Diego, to the endless Trump roadside posters in the countryside outside the urban centres in the traditional Democratic strongholds of both California and Oregon, I flew back to the UK after three weeks convinced that Trump really could win. His continued reference to Brexit as the catalyst for change in America was striking.

While I was away, I took a call from the outgoing CEO of TheCityUK, Chris Cummings. Chris and I had worked together for the entire decade as he had built the body into the leading voice for the sector. He had a new challenge for me:

would Cicero be able to provide political support for a new group called the European Financial Services Chairs Advisory Committee (EFSCAC)? Basically, it would be a meeting place for the chairs of the mighty EU and UK banks based in London to caucus and provide both the UK government and the EU with a clear view on the way ahead. It sounded just the sort of place where Cicero ought to play – so I readily agreed.

When I got back to my desk in London, I heard that Charles Roxburgh, the lead Treasury official with oversight of financial services, had been asking around the City about what finance would like to see post-Brexit. His question appeared on the face of it to be rather simple: what did you like about the EU regime that you would want the UK to adopt in its rules and regulations for a post-Brexit world – and what didn't you like that you would like to drop? But I heard from senior Treasury officials that Roxburgh's mission was rather fruitless. Through the summer of 2016 he could find no consistent view and was met with a viscerally angry response from business leaders, who wanted to put EU membership of the single market back on the table. The initial response was angry and – in hindsight – delusional.

Worse still, when I started to advise the EFSCAC group, I found the job initially almost impossible. Because of the lack of a consistent, single lobbying viewpoint, the meetings and their minutes and strategy papers were being leaked to the newspapers within minutes of meetings ending. The joint chairs of the group, Barclays chair John McFarlane and Santander chair Baroness Shriti Vadera, had to issue an edict to calm the waters. Briefings and minutes were sent out with watermarked versions to seek out who was leaking what to whom. The trust built up over years between business and Whitehall was rapidly eroding.

What had become clear as a result of Brexit was that many businesses had located in the UK because of the stability of the UK political regime alongside the EU single market passport. Now that the UK was filled with political instability and the passport was no longer likely to be on offer, the myriad of different business models and foreign ownerships with different 'motherships' located outside the EU were on show for all to see. Maintaining consensus was going to be very difficult to achieve. In the early weeks after the Brexit vote, securing a single voice for business was nigh-on impossible.

6

WHAT DOES THERESA WANT?

Business always calls for certainty from politicians. They have been doing so ever since I have been doing this job. But it's a forlorn hope. Politicians will always seize the main chance to stay in power and get closer to the electorate – every time. It's got worse, and business has not helped itself either. In the decade since the financial crisis, the gulf between CEO and average worker pay levels and the debate on corporate tax has done nothing other than shred trust and confidence in many of our major private sector institutions. In so many ways business has helped itself but not helped its cause. And our politicians – extremists or centrists – have railed hard and acted accordingly.

When it came to Brexit, most businesses had found themselves on the losing side. It was not a place they were used to being in. As Cameron left office and Theresa May walked into Downing Street my job of advising business was focused on two key questions: what kind of government would Theresa May lead and what would be her approach towards Brexit?

On the first question she had little time to set out her stall. The Tory leadership election had been cut short by Andrea

Leadsom's decision to pull out of the final race. Only May's putative policy around workers on boards had been sketched out, and then only in campaigning poetry rather than in detailed prose. Little else was evident. Neither politicians nor business folk had seen the future Prime Minister tested in a campaign. There was little to hang on to. The media started turning to the back catalogue of blogs from Nick Timothy, her policy Svengali, on the influential ConservativeHome website. So obsessed were political watchers with analysing his words that by the end of summer 2016, Timothy had himself become the story for most businesses and political watchers wanting to understand what May would do. The plan to set up new grammar schools was the most eye-catching example of his impact on May – a policy destined to hit the Whitehall dustbin almost as quickly as it was announced. It was an old Tory favourite that harked back to a different era but was designed to appeal to aspiration too.

For inward investors, the more significant announcement was the halting – for a painful few months – of a major investment into the UK's nuclear power sector by a joint Franco-Chinese consortium. The message this sent out just weeks after the UK had voted for Brexit was intended for domestic consumption. On coming into office, Theresa May had immediately sacked the most pro-Chinese minister a UK government had ever seen in former Chancellor George Osborne. He had assiduously cultivated inward investment into the UK and had focused much of his effort on Chinese relations to boost UK performance. He also believed that the long-termism of the Chinese was just what Britain needed after years of myopic short-term business investment. May, with her chief of staff, was going to send out different smoke signals to inward investors: less welcoming and totally inscrutable.

It was not just Chinese investors who were angered in those initial weeks. The long-standing hold-up on building a third runway at Heathrow had been an ongoing source of tension for business throughout the Cameron years. He had outsourced the problem to RBS chair Sir Howard Davies to undertake a review of Britain's airport capacity. Free from any political calculus around the marginal constituencies near Heathrow, and rigorously independent-minded, Sir Howard came down on the side of building the third runway, but the decision would be kicked into the long grass as a result of the Brexit drama. When May arrived in Downing Street, the intense lobbying from Heathrow's Spanish shareholder Ferrovial started again in earnest – only to be met with further months of delay. When Transport Secretary Chris Grayling did eventually give the green light two years later, on 5 June 2018, another signal had been sent that international investors would just have to bide their time. In any case, the new May government was consumed by Brexit.

George Parker, political editor at the *Financial Times*, has a different kind of ringside seat to mine; he sits in Westminster writing about politics for the business world. Given his perspective, we talk a lot. He told me:

Theresa May's decision to systematically disengage with business after becoming Prime Minister was profoundly shocking for corporate UK, which had become accustomed to the open-door policy offered to FTSE 100 chief

executives by Cameron and Osborne. One of her top advisers – Nick Timothy – in her first year as Prime Minister
upbraided me for suggesting that Mrs May had deliberately sidelined business. But how else can you explain what
happened?

Back in September 2016, the new Prime Minister dissolved
the business advisory group created by her predecessor. She
claimed she wanted to engage with business in a 'different
way', by which she meant – it turned out – barely engaging
at all. When there was a dialogue with groups like the CBI,
it was frosty in the extreme. Juergen Maier, chief executive
of Siemens UK, is one of the UK's major inward investors.
From trains to Britain's energy needs, his business strides
across the UK economy. Speaking to me for this book, he
told me: 'I am not seeing enough appetite from politicians
to invest in manufacturing or infrastructure or tech or to fire
up the fourth industrial revolution.' But BBC political editor
Laura Kuenssberg is clear that May had her own strong
views on most issues, that she read the evidence and was not
swayed by lobbying. Kuenssberg told me: 'The PM had her
own mind. The idea that the advisers were manipulating her
was for the birds.'

This also reflected May's preference for making a break
with the Cameron era and her natural focus on home affairs
rather than the economy. George Parker said: 'Nick Clegg
once told me he could not remember a single significant
contribution by May on the economy during the five years
of the coalition, other than to push a restrictive line on
immigration.'

Parker also reflected on the nature of the engagement which did take place:

Downing Street would always protest that she held dinners with CEOs but those who attended them said they were social occasions where 'talking shop' was frowned upon. One person who attended the rare soirées told me: 'She deliberately invited spouses to the dinners so that people felt uncomfortable talking about business issues. It was made clear that this was not the point of the events.'

Her decision was partly strategic. Being the 'party of business' was at odds with the strategy being pursued by Timothy to push the Tory brand into working-class areas such as the Birmingham suburbs, where he grew up. So there was a deliberate policy to stand away from the major corporates. However, it was the second question that business most inquired about. How would the May government deal with Brexit? To gain an insight into the decision making, I had a stroke of luck. Usually, the government machine makes itself an impenetrable morass for anyone trying to find out what is really going on inside. Finding the right person to talk to on the issue you want to discuss is like finding a needle in a haystack sometimes.

However, on the week Theresa May entered Downing Street, I spotted a *Financial Times* story which indicated that John Godfrey was set to enter government as head of the policy unit. I knew someone with that name. John and I had first met over thirty years earlier as members of the Scottish Young Conservatives in the mid-1980s, and we had kept in touch on and off over the years. John had spent some time as Douglas Hurd's special adviser at the Home Office under John Major. More recently, we knew each other when he became director of communications for Legal & General, the largest shareholder in the London market. John had got to know Nick Timothy in that role, as L&G had become one of the most effective lobbyists in the corporate sector. Its CEO, Nigel Wilson, used political campaigning techniques to call for more investment in affordable homes and the UK's infrastructure needs. He was right most of the time and his calls struck a chord with Timothy. On securing victory in the Tory leadership campaign, Timothy had asked Godfrey to become the head of the policy unit.

When I read the story naming John as the new policy chief, I texted him and asked: 'The John Godfrey in the *FT* today being named as the new head of the policy unit – is it you?' Within seconds he was back to me: 'Don't be so cheeky. Of course, it is me. I'm having to wind up rapidly at L&G and will be in No. 10 next week.' We agreed to meet.

Speaking to me for this book, John said: 'It was a shock to get the call. I had not been expecting it. But I saw this as a major opportunity to serve at a momentous time. Also, from what I knew of the PM's agenda and Nick's approach, I was excited by the prospect.' Godfrey had got to know Timothy reasonably well, but he suggested that they were far from close confidants. While the Brexit strategy would be managed by Timothy and Fiona Hill, Godfrey would be free to roam across the domestic agenda.

I went into Downing Street later that summer to meet John. He looked slightly ill at ease in his office. The minimalist, rather incongruous angular furniture and art from the government 'collection' left in something of a rush by David Cameron's own policy chief, Camilla Cavendish, was still in place. It was not very John. It looked like the contents of The Conran Shop had been left in the Georgian townhouse that is No. 10. I noted later that after a year in office John hadn't had the time to replace it. We talked about the approach towards business and he indicated that he wanted to keep the dialogue going. Of course, in the months to come I would discover that his door was one of the very few to be kept open in No. 10 to business dialogue. When we talked ahead of this book, Godfrey said:

> It is not that the Prime Minister or her key advisers were anti-business – if anything they were anti-corporatist. There was a feeling that during the Cameron–Osborne era there had been a revolving door and access was very easy for the biggest businesses, whereas what Theresa wanted to do was be accessible to business as required but particularly to small business. But with the benefit of hindsight she could have been seen to be more open with big business.

In mid-September 2016 I was invited to the leaving do of Simon Walker, the outgoing director general of the business organisation the Institute of Directors (IoD). Simon had done an outstanding job in that role and had navigated the EU referendum better than other business organisations. The CBI was being regularly attacked by government ministers for still not coming to terms with the result of the referendum, and the British Chambers of Commerce was still recovering from their former director general John Longworth's spectacular exit in the middle of the referendum campaign, after he backed the Leave cause at his annual conference without telling his own board beforehand. But Simon Walker's IoD was still standing and had become an important interlocutor for government. Through the campaign, the IoD had simply made clear that its members would like to see the UK remain in the EU but had avoided becoming politicised in the process.

Simon was something of a mentor to me. He had worked in the No. 10 policy unit under John Major and had built a successful career in lobbying. He later worked at Buckingham Palace and had impeccable networking skills across the Whitehall and Westminster machine. The IoD was lucky to have him and he would be a big loss to their operations. As things turned out, within a year of his leaving, the IoD was to be engulfed in a very public corporate governance row and a declining membership – Simon's departure had a bigger impact than any of us could have imagined. So the question still exists to this day: who is the most effective voice for the business sector with government and opposition? It is still an unanswered question. While the CBI – and, latterly, the IoD – has made heavy weather of the Brexit debate, the British Chambers of Commerce has had something of a renaissance since that summer of 2016 as one of the more effective voices closer to communities for which they speak, by posing concrete questions to policymakers and business.

The rhetoric of the Brexit debate had tried to suggest there was a division between small and large businesses too. It was not fair or accurate to either side. Most businesses, large and small, did not want to see disruption. Talking to me for this book, Adam Marshall, director general of the British Chambers of Commerce, said:

> I reject artificial attempts to divide large and small business into two different camps. Business is not monolithic – companies have a variety of different views, but most are pragmatic, and that's why most businesses have argued for an economically sensible approach to Brexit. The political debate has all gone on at 30,000 feet – whereas businesses, whatever their view, want and deserve engagement on the details at ground level.

When I walked into that leaving do at the IoD's grand Pall Mall headquarters, I could see the impact of Simon's lobbying power and his ability to allow the IoD to talk to both sides of the new Conservative government and inside the ongoing Tory Brexit schism. Half of the new Cabinet had turned up to say goodbye to him. The new Chancellor and former Remain backer Philip Hammond was there, alongside the new Trade Secretary and committed Leaver Liam Fox. Business Secretary Greg Clark – another Remainer – mingled at one end of the room and new Brexit Secretary David Davis mingled at the other end.

In the midst of all this the Westminster lobby was out in force. I spent some time with George Parker, and we marvelled at Simon's ecumenical politics assembled in the room. But I also spotted John Godfrey with his deputy Will Tanner. Will had cut his teeth at centre-right think tank Reform but

I had not seen him since he went to work for Theresa May at the Home Office. Tanner is a very tall figure and was easy to spot in the crowded, gilded IoD reception room in the heart of London's clubland on Pall Mall.

John and Will wanted to brief me on the forthcoming boardroom reforms that May had promised as the only major announcement in the all too brief Tory leadership campaign. This was set to be a signature policy. I listened to them positively and politely, but I wanted to move the conversation on. As everyone had a glass in hand, I took my chance and asked John the question I had been wanting to ask him all summer: 'What is the PM aiming for with Brexit?' By now Will had left us to talk one to one.

'Remember, Iain – she was a Remainer,' said Godfrey.

'I know,' I said. 'But not a very demonstrative one. She played the politics of the campaign a blinder to become the Tory leader.' John smiled.

'Business will hear a lot of things that it really doesn't want to hear in the next couple of years. But – at the end of the day – the Prime Minister wants to secure the softest Brexit possible.'

Our brief conversation ended, but I had gained the most important insight into the Prime Minister's approach since she had entered office. The next day I shared that briefing on an unnamed basis with a range of major businesses. It seemed to calm people down. When I was to see the final version of the Withdrawal Agreement two years later, in December 2018, it all made sense. The deal was as close as possible to that 'softest' Brexit that John had believed Theresa May was aiming for. But John's warning was also right – the months ahead were to see a range of pronouncements and commitments made by the Prime Minister that would shake business to its core and start the process of planning for a hard Brexit in earnest.

When we spoke later for this book, Godfrey explained: 'Back then the idea of transitionals weren't baked in, so the idea of an exit that limited economic damage was a bit different to today's hard/soft dilemma. However, the PM was clear that she thought a unique UK solution, that is not Norway, nor Switzerland, was possible and desirable.'

He continued: 'I think that sums up what we were thinking, at the time, in No. 10. Certainly, what I was thinking, which was the ideal scenario was to deliver it while keeping economic growth running throughout.'

So, was there was a Brexit strategy?

'I would characterise it more as an inclination than a strategy', said Godfrey. '[Nick Timothy] might well have described it as strategy. The nearest thing we had to strategy in No. 10 was what she said on the doorstep on day one.'

I also spoke to Cabinet minister Amber Rudd – May's first Home Secretary for most of her tenure and a prominent player in the Remain campaign – who told me: 'I believe the PM did have a strategy – it was to protect the economy and to protect the union. When she first became PM, she travelled to all four parts of the union within hours of entering No. 10.'

However, those who had been thrown out of No. 10 as a result of Brexit are a lot less charitable. Craig Oliver suggests: 'Her entire strategy seemed to be: appease the hardliner Brexiteers at all costs. She feared a Corn Laws moment for the Tories. In the end, Brexit came into contact with reality

– and the people she'd appeased didn't want to hear their perfect vision was a pipe dream.'

In the end that was the viewpoint that became the overriding one for business. Because of the Sphinx-like behaviour from No. 10, business had neither the time nor the inclination to become mind-readers of the Prime Minister's every nuance. All they could do was listen to the words she uttered in public and, on this, John Godfrey was to be proved right. Business did hate the words.

Like most lobbyists, I headed off to the Tory conference in 2016. (I agreed with the sentiment of friends like Tim Montgomerie that party conferences had ceased to be political events and had become a money-spinning corporate fundraising exercise which had sucked the life out of them, but as head of one of the UK's largest lobbying firms I had little choice but to attend.) And, as for most other political geeks, the Sunday morning news shows are required viewing in my house. In fact, I find *The Andrew Marr Show* in particular a brilliant way of 'short-circuiting' the political strategy for the entire conference week ahead. On Sunday 2 October 2016, Theresa May sat down to be interviewed by Andrew Marr in Birmingham. The preparations for these interviews are meticulous. It is usually the biggest politics show audience of the political week, second only to BBC's *Question Time*. Politicians who want to deliver a key message usually tip off the show's producers well in advance. At the time, Robbie Gibb – later to enter Downing Street in 2017 – was still atop the show as its editor.

Marr asked the Prime Minister about her plans for Brexit. Without missing a beat, Theresa May told the nation that

Article 50 would be triggered no later than Easter 2017; most political watchers took this to mean leaving the EU on 31 March 2019. She had dug herself out of the potential bear trap of the conference week ahead. If she hadn't made clear her intention to push the button on Article 50, the Brexiteers would have had a field day on the fringe and derailed the conference – something Tory leaders had been enduring since the early 1990s. However, businesses were stunned. The government had not given any indication about what kind of Brexit we were heading towards. Would single market membership be on offer? Or was the aim World Trade Organization (WTO) terms? The clock was now ticking on the most important economic negotiations since the Second World War, and no one had any clue about what would happen next.

When most business leaders arrived in Birmingham the next day, they were in shock. They headed into the Tory business conference – a side event around the main political conference where a line-up of ministers gather every year to talk to and mingle with the corporate guests. The rattled attendees were asking endless questions about what was on the horizon, but they didn't get many detailed answers. The relationship with the corporate sector, which was already at a low point, had sunk even lower. But there was worse to come.

The final speech at the Tory conference is always the leader's opportunity to rally the troops; Birmingham 2016 was no exception. Tory activists – at least 70 per cent of whom had supported Brexit – were already fired up by the Prime Minister's commitment to trigger Article 50 in just six months. They leapt to their feet when Theresa May entered the Birmingham Symphony Hall. She proceeded to set out – as new Prime Ministers do – her personal political credo. She repeated the mantras she had offered when walking into Downing Street in July 2016: social mobility and opportunity for all were the watchwords. It was an understandable and coherent approach.

Then she offered some 'blue meat' to the hall, who – as I have argued – had grown apart from the world of big business and the corporate elite over the past two decades. She labelled those who turn up at the big annual economic conferences like the World Economic Forum in Davos as 'citizens of nowhere'. The room loved it, but any business leaders in the room – there were just a few – were in torture. Many of them had made the UK their home and had brought business to and built business in this country. The pound began to plummet before the Prime Minister had even sat down, and by the end of the day it had fallen to a three-year low against the euro by over 1 per cent to €1.14. The markets had assumed that – after triggering Article 50 and by using hardcore Brexiteer rhetoric – her strategy was to head for a hard Brexit. It was the worst day for the currency since the Brexit vote itself. Leaving the conference hall, I bumped into *Financial Times* chief political correspondent Jim Pickard and his colleague, City editor Jonathan Ford. 'What did you think?' asked Jim.

'It's terrible. I know what the PM is doing and they are not listening to business right now as a deliberate strategy to correct what happened before,' I said. 'There is a "la-la-la-la" moment going on. Financial services companies are not the top priority. This is all about the message that they want to govern differently [to Cameron]. Finance needs to learn how to talk differently to this government.' Later that day my words appeared online and the next day in print in Jim's write-up of the business reaction to the speech.

Over the coming days, the wider business reaction was swift. Normally businesses like to do their lobbying privately, but this was different. I had known Colm Kelleher, president of the investment bank Morgan Stanley, for some time. I had worked with his business. He is thoughtful and respected across the corporate world and – as an Irish citizen – he was a prime example of a foreign national who had made his life in the UK and built Morgan Stanley's operations here. Clearly, Colm Kelleher could not contain his private thoughts any more. He put them into print in *The Times* on 31 October 2016, writing:

> Suddenly a 'hard' Brexit is more than a theoretical possibility ... While it is tempting to dismiss talk of a hard Brexit as posturing, history is replete with bluffs gone wrong. Not surprisingly the market has reacted to the rhetoric by sending the pound down. Nowhere is the sense of a looming cliff greater than in the financial sector. On Brexit day one, all UK-based financial firms ... will lose their passporting rights.[18]

The damage with the business world had been done, and it was intentional. 'The speech was designed for the room,' John Godfrey later told me in November 2016, sitting in his office in Downing Street with the angular white furniture still firmly in place. I said: 'I know, John – but how naive was

---

18 Colm Kelleher, 'London is a European public good as well as a British one', *The Times*, 31 October 2016.

that. Markets listen to speeches too, you know.' Godfrey acknowledged the problem and agreed that better signposting was needed for business and markets in the months ahead. 'I will do everything I can,' he said.

Recalling the events for this book, Godfrey told me:

I think businesses hated the 'citizens of nowhere' line, which was a complete attack on corporatism. This reflected a belief by Nick [Timothy] that the Conservative Party had become detached from people it had historically represented. Were we working for small businesses? Were we working for communities? Business was unbelievably thin-skinned about this. This was a party conference speech; you would have thought that business would have rolled with the punches.

I also spoke to former IoD deputy director of policy Andy Silvester, who explained further:

To be honest, the relationship soured from the 2016 party conference. The new Home Secretary, Amber Rudd, was drawing up plans for registers of foreign workers and the PM was having a pop at citizens of nowhere. Maybe business had grown used to being indulged by Cameron and Osborne. The contrast was striking.

However, he suggests that business didn't help itself either:

You can understand why the mood in No. 10 towards business groups wasn't exactly warm and fuzzy. Every time they opened the papers, they saw lobby groups taking pot-shots at the very time they were trying to build a co-alition for a business-friendly Brexit behind the scenes. Meanwhile, we were pulling our punches on Corbyn.

In fact, there is direct evidence of the hostility the Prime Minister's advisers had shown business leaders in the immediate aftermath of the referendum. Before the party conference in 2016 – May's first as leader – the CBI was summoned to No. 10 for what can only be described as a full-frontal verbal dressing-down from the Prime Minister's closest confidants. Speaking to me for this book, Paul Drechsler – who was CBI president at the time – told me that he and director general Carolyn Fairbairn were asked to come to Downing Street for a 'discussion'. He went on: 'I and Carolyn found ourselves in No. 10 being screamed at by her top advisers. I had never been spoken to like that by anyone in my forty years in business. There was no respect.'

Others were to find a similar experience across the May government. TheCityUK and Barclays chairman John Mc-Farlane told me: 'David Davis – and many of his colleagues in government – believed the City, as we had done in the past, would sort itself out, and everything would end up fine. They weren't worried about us.' Drechsler adds: 'The teams around May have been awful. Davis was the worst. He simply didn't listen to a single word.'

Weeks later, I went to see a very senior official in the Treasury to reflect on events and provide them with a perspective about the looming relocations into the EU and away from the UK that were being considered by firms. They told me:

The conference speech by the PM was a disaster from the point of view of what we are trying to do here. We are trying to calm people down. Markets freaked out and I know business leaders have done so too. We know firms have to make plans to ensure they can continue to operate after Brexit. But can you just ensure that they do so with the minimum of fuss – otherwise the politics will get even more difficult.

While Treasury officials and John Godfrey were doing their best to calm things down, some ministers were on an entirely different script altogether (if – as a result of the inscrutable No. 10 'strategy' – they even knew what the script was at all). One of the early backers of Theresa May's leadership campaign was Simon Kirby, the MP for Brighton Kemptown since 2010. A May loyalist, he had been a parliamentary private secretary to several ministers, and served as a whip, but had never been a minister himself. I was told while writing this book that Theresa May resorted to an old style of appointing her government: she would appoint the Cabinet while her then chief whip Gavin Williamson had appointed the rest of the government based on his own intelligence on each candidates' capabilities.

Kirby was appointed City minister in July 2016. The job is one of the most difficult in the junior ranks of government. It is complex, as you are overseeing the top-performing economic sector in the UK economy and political responsibility over its highly complex regulatory structure. Some ministers, like Ed Balls and Nicky Morgan, are deeply interested in their work, successful and use this role as a political springboard – others are not quite so lucky. Kirby proved to be in the second category. He got a reputation for being unable to firmly command his brief by the civil servants around him. You know that's the case when Whitehall starts to issue edicts before a meeting that 'the minister is very busy and will only be available for his fifteen-minute speech and will have to leave immediately without taking any questions'. Having observed this over many years, this is usually Whitehall-speak for: 'The minister is really not very good at his job so we need to ensure he sticks rigidly to the script and we need to get him out of the room as quickly as possible without making any gaffes.'

Privately, I knew this to be the case. One of my colleagues had gone in to meet Kirby earlier that autumn with an international business at the imposing Treasury building opposite St James's Park. Kirby – who was a rather friendly chap – greeted everyone and mentioned that senior Treasury mandarin Charles Roxburgh had accompanied him to the meeting. He told the room: 'I've brought Charles with me because I want to make sure I don't say anything stupid.' I'm told Roxburgh smiled sheepishly. At least Kirby was self-aware if nothing else.

On 8 November 2016, I was due to give my latest political weather forecast to TheCityUK advisory group, which comprised the senior captains of the UK finance sector: HSBC's Douglas Flint, Barclays' John MacFarlane, Morgan Stanley's Colm Kelleher and around thirty other chiefs would all be there around a massive table, which can only be described as resembling one of those international summits you see with world leaders all posing for the cameras. Giant screens surrounded the meeting to allow the audience to see my presentation. It was the day of the US presidential election and I used my time to talk about the prospects of a Trump presidency. I made the right call on that, at least. But topping the bill for the start of the meeting was an address from City minister Kirby. When the chair of the meeting made clear that Kirby was 'very busy' and would be speaking for fifteen minutes with time to take one question, I smiled and caught the eye of John McFarlane, who winked back at me. He knew what that meant.

The speech was a disaster. We were in the height of the excitement of Ed Balls – one of his predecessors as City minister – appearing on *Strictly Come Dancing* to some success. Kirby, who had run an entertainment business in Brighton before he entered Parliament and clearly thought he could step on the stage himself, went entirely off the Treasury-prepared script and attempted a long-running joke about former City ministers being great tap dancers. At this momentous time in the UK's history, I watched as Flint, McFarlane and Kelleher struggled to keep their faces straight in disbelief. When Kirby left the room, they let rip. This was the most dismal City minister in years, they said, and urged that we needed to be talking directly to Philip Hammond as Chancellor. They were right.

In autumn 2016, after the party conference dramas, I was invited to an event put together by some of the most prominent Brexiteers. Weeks earlier, the new BrexitCentral blog – based in the same location as the right-wing pressure group the TaxPayers' Alliance, which had spawned other pro-Brexit initiatives and was funded by prominent Brexiteers – had been launched by former BBC and *Daily Telegraph* reporter and ConHome blogger Jonathan Isaby. I had known Jonathan for years. When the blog launched, I wrote a column saying that, while I had voted for Remain, we needed to make the best of Brexit and – for me – that meant ensuring we achieved the softest landing possible for our economy.

I think as a result of writing the blog, I was subsequently asked to attend an event packed out with some of the most prominent Brexiteer backers from the business sector, plus two Remain supporters in the form of myself and Michael Spencer. I found myself in a subterranean room deep in the bowels of the Bulgari Hotel in Knightsbridge listening to former Australian premier John Howard. Howard had been a supporter of Brexit and was in London to talk up a future trade deal with Australia. While he was a most entertaining speaker, he was only the warm-up act for a panel discussion with DExEU Secretary David Davis and International Trade Secretary Liam Fox. They arrived very late and John Howard had to 'tap dance' for some considerable time before they arrived. The reason for their late arrival was obvious when they stepped onto the stage looking rather exhausted.

'Sorry we are late,' said Davis. 'We have just been in one of the Cabinet subcommittees on Brexit and it was a very long meeting. Some of this is proving to be fiendishly hard to do.' This was not the breezy, self-confident Brexit campaigner but now a Secretary of State with one of the hardest jobs in British post-war history. The reaction of the room was instructive. In their questions, most of the audience indicated that Davis and Fox could make life much easier for themselves by leaving the EU without a deal on WTO terms. To be fair to both, they pushed back on this idea and said they were aiming to get a deal, but it was clear to me that a whole host of Brexiteers would continue to foment this idea in political circles. It was merely the start of the rows to come.

7

BUSINESS GETS A PLAN – IT'S CALLED LANCASTER HOUSE

I think everyone in business and politics was pleased to see 2016 end. It had been an exhausting year in which relationships had been strained or even broken for ever. Everyone was shattered and there were not many signs on the horizon that businesses knew where we were heading.

The long-expected government White Paper on boardroom and corporate governance reform, which Theresa May had been talking about before she entered Downing Street, was launched in November 2016. While many business leaders were sceptical about the idea of workers on boards and a radical reshaping of the corporate landscape, I was a lot more sanguine. As a lobbyist, I have long recognised that there is a need for give and take in the relationship between government and business. I judged that giving a broad welcome to the overall direction of the government's plans for reform might help to underpin a better day-to-day relationship.

I reached out to No. 10 to get some advance briefing on

the plans. Tom Swarbrick, who now hosts a lively late-night chat show on LBC Radio, was in the Downing Street machine spinning away. He called me with the details and asked if I would be prepared to front some of the conversations with the media. As a former journalist myself, I have always enjoyed this and agreed to do so. When I read the plans, they were not nearly as radical as had been initially proposed. There had been a great debate between No. 10 and Greg Clark at the Department for Business, Energy and Industrial Strategy (BEIS), who has seen himself as a champion for business throughout his tenure. Hammond too was a brake on radical reform.

The plans did not mandate change for smaller firms and it was not made compulsory for workers to sit directly on the boards of large firms, but what the proposals did do was provide business with a more effective way of shaping a better conversation between workers and boards, which I believed was part of the answer to the disconnection that had built up between the two. This disconnection was – and perhaps remains – a primary reason that many boards just didn't understand what was going on in the real world, as well as for the dislocation in society. It's why businesses often said to me: 'I don't know anyone that voted for Brexit...' The plans were also immeasurably better than what was on offer from Labour, which was already talking about ripping up contractual rights. With the advance briefing from government, I put pen to paper and wrote a column for *City AM*, the leading City of London business tabloid that had grown in stature under the editorship of

Allister Heath and was now under the nib of the brilliant Christian May.[19]

My column set out to welcome the reforms, counteracting the many business organisations that were giving the proposals a cool response. My purpose was clear: business really had to show that it had learned some lessons from the politics of 2016, that it was listening to the shop floor as much as the boardroom or to investors, and that it was ready to embrace reform. I found myself doing a round of TV news interviews as one of the sole business voices prepared to welcome reform. But I had a strategy here – it was to provide some legitimacy for government to sit down, engage and talk meaningfully with the corporate world. The trenches between business and government had just become too deep; everyone needed to climb out, and No. 10 had to open the door once again to meaningful dialogue, but the real question was: is that going to be possible?

Just before the end of 2016 something else happened. There was reason to provide some hope to both the politicians and the business class. An idea was placed on the table which looked like a way of solving the problem of losing the passport for the dominant financial services sector. It was called 'enhanced equivalence'.

Now this book is not an academic text or a management book – it's more of a diary and reflections on the events which have shaped and soured the relations and language between politics and business through the Brexit journey – but in

---

19 Iain Anderson, 'Business should embrace the government's radical corporate governance proposals to strike a better relationship with the public', *City AM*, 26 November 2016.

subsequent chapters we will look at some of the detail of the issues involved. One of the problems across the entire debate – a problem which led to neither side listening to the other – was that there had been no substantial policy proposal from Brexiteers to address the services problem. With three-quarters of the UK economy based on services rather than goods output and with financial services being the UK's leading export earner, no one had cracked the issue of how to replicate the single market passporting rights. Much of the EU has used the City of London as the gateway to capital raising. It is the closest global market for EU governments to trade eurobonds and their own sovereign debt, and it is the most efficient place for European businesses like Lufthansa and Siemens to raise debt. But when I or my team at Cicero asked Brexiteer ministers for their detailed plans on services, and when we asked the UK government for their detailed plans for financial services, the initial silence was deafening. They usually asked the question back – what ideas do you have? The argument around WTO terms for goods can be made, but for services the arguments would be distinctly more complex.

But, as Colm Kelleher of Morgan Stanley argued in his *Times* piece of 31 October 2016, the withdrawal of the passport would prove to be a huge disincentive for financial firms to remain in London after Brexit day one. Around this time, the work of City lawyer Barney Reynolds started to come to prominence. Reynolds had been one of the few City lawyers specialising in financial services in the 1990s and had gone on to build a large practice at US law firm Shearman and Sterling's London office. Reynolds had been called upon by Cameron's team back in 2015 to be sounded out on the pre-referendum EU renegotiations. Cameron had wanted to secure the rights of the City of London in future EU financial sector laws against the likely power of eurozone countries who would use qualified majority votes to work together to erode London's powers. Reynolds had worked on some thinking to send to the UK government on the carve-out that Cameron eventually obtained as part of his deal with the EU in early spring 2016 before he called the referendum itself.

Just a few days after the Brexit vote in June 2016, Reynolds got on a plane to Washington to speak to the annual gathering of international bankers called the Institute for International Finance. Like many others at the time, Reynolds encountered a room of liberal financiers mesmerised by the Brexit result, unable to understand it, and now concerned about the likelihood of Trump in the White House – but not focusing on the solutions required.

Speaking to me for this book, Reynolds said:

I had never been involved with politics and had not campaigned in the EU referendum but I believed that we simply had to get on with putting on the table some practical legislative solutions to what had just happened. I started from the point of view that the financial passport was simply *not* going to be available to us as – inevitably – we would be a 'third country' outside the EU.

With that in mind, Reynolds started to sketch out in his speech to those international bankers his concept of 'enhanced' equivalence. Equivalence is one which is well known in international treaties and, simply put, it's the idea that one trading bloc will recognise the other's rules and regulations if the other side adopts a broadly equivalent legal and regulatory approach. The flaw in the plan, according to its detractors, is that equivalent arrangements can be unpicked at will by politicians as bellicose rhetoric turns into a trade war. Reynolds's plan was to enhance that equivalence by creating binding arbitration structures that would – as far as possible – remove that day-to-day political interference. In November 2016, he published a paper with the centre-right think tank Politeia, which had been working on Brexit solutions in a number of arenas.[20] The 'Blueprint for Brexit' certainly caught the eye and got some politicians off the hook. At last, someone had given them their script. Detailed legislative ideas which they and officials could actually work with were now on offer as opposed to the generalised wringing of hands which had been in place for months from commerce and politics. He told me: 'The reaction from the UK government, from the Treasury and from DExEU was immediate and positive. I also took calls from the EU Commission and many member states looking to hear more. Financial firms – especially the banks – wanted to hear a lot more.'

So Reynolds packed his bags and headed around Europe to talk to policymakers and business about how enhanced equivalence might work. One of those who caught the excitement of the Reynolds plan was John McFarlane, the then chair of Barclays and TheCityUK. John invited me to come to talk to the final Barclays board meeting of 2016 about the politics ahead. Before I spoke, his deputy chair and City

---

20 Barnabas Reynolds, 'A Blueprint for Brexit: The Future of Global Financial Services and Markets in the UK', Politeia.

grandee Sir Gerry Grimstone updated the board on his latest trip to Asia, where he had accompanied the Prime Minister on the latest trade delegation. It seemed the relationship with the Chinese had warmed up considerably on the trip, but Sir Gerry reflected that the Prime Minister's key advisers remained very distant from business and wanted to protect her from being seen to get too close to the corporations on the prime ministerial plane.

I talked to the Barclays board, who – like everyone else in 2016 – just wanted Christmas to come early. Like most FTSE boards, it comprises a range of interests and around a third of those around the table had flown in from other parts of the world – so there was some UK politics decoding to do. I told them to be ready for more hard language from the May government and not a lot of 'leaning in' towards commerce in 2017. We also reflected on the election of Donald Trump. The language against 'global' business was only going to intensify when the new President took office. When it came to questions, I was able to talk to them about my sense that the Prime Minister was aiming for a soft Brexit, but that they would have to hear things that would continue to unsettle them. We then talked of Brexit, and John McFarlane referred to the Barney Reynolds plan. I told the board that it was the only plan on the table right now and that government was taking it seriously. However, I said that both UK and EU politics remained a problem for the plan and the industry needed to find its own way through and come up with its own ideas, rather than continuing to wring its hands or hope it would all go away and that single market access would continue to be on offer.

The signs that the government machine had learned the lessons of the party conference car crash with business were there to see when we entered 2017. Better signalling of intent was to be the order of the day. The Prime Minister agreed to do a set-piece interview at the start of the year to launch the brand new *Sophy Ridge on Sunday* show on Sky News. The BBC was highly miffed – normally Andrew Marr got that privilege. He would have to wait another week. The interview was to take place around ten days before May would give her Lancaster House speech in which she would lay out the details of her approach to the negotiations.

May unpacked her detailed approach towards Brexit for the first time. Governed by her own red lines on immigration, which she had articulated for some years as Home Secretary, she signalled (but did not divulge all the specifics) that the UK was not likely to be in the single market or the customs union. Inevitably, the business organisations let out their anger immediately; on the Monday when markets opened, the pound fell again. But by the time the Prime Minister spoke at Lancaster House on 17 January 2017, markets and business had priced in the new approach. Now most businesses did not like the approach one bit, but at least there was a benchmark for which to plan ahead. They knew now what they faced.

The Lancaster House speech set out the Prime Minister's 'Plan for Britain' – which were her key priorities in the upcoming Brexit negotiations. The speech ruled out membership of the single market and full membership of the customs union, while promising to negotiate towards the 'freest possible trade' with European countries after leaving the EU. The speech also set out the primary concern of controlling migration after Brexit, and Theresa May argued the mantra she was to repeat over and over again, that 'no deal is better than a bad deal'. Everyone in business focused in on the words. Ruling out membership of the customs union was the kind of political fudge we would all grow used to and tired of. It was interpreted by some as the mechanism for the UK to take advantage of the trade opportunity ahead and by others as opening up the prospect to the softest deal possible. This triangulation was to consume the lobbying for another eighteen months until the fateful Chequers Cabinet away day in the summer of 2018 when the Tory Party Cabinet truce bust wide open.

My calendar filled up once again with FTSE boards wanting to hear more about the Lancaster House approach and if there was any chance of the Prime Minister changing her red lines (I had to quickly disabuse the business leaders who asked that question) and quickly my work and the work of Cicero Group moved into a new phase. The campaign by business to keep the UK in the single market with full passport access had failed – it was now time to seek out new solutions. It was also time to start planning in earnest for life as a 'third country' trading with the EU. In retrospect, business and its lobbying should have moved faster into that place.

By the time Article 50 was invoked on 29 March 2017, business had started to focus on the planning and preparation to take economic activities out of the UK in order to secure their own passporting rights. If the government would not or could not listen and adapt, business needed to take its own destiny into its own hands. The lobbying was done.

8

YOUR GDP NOT MY GDP

One of the most memorable stories from the EU referendum was told by Professor Anand Menon, the brilliantly engaging public intellectual who runs The UK in a Changing Europe think tank from King's College London. Menon – more than most think-tankers – has taken the time to get under the bonnet of why the UK and the EU drifted apart over the past decade, in particular from a political and socio-economic point of view. His story is one which I have used with countless boardrooms over the past few years when they fail to understand how Brexit happened and why – despite the quagmire of Westminster politics – the trenches for Leave remain so deep.

The story is best encapsulated in this excerpt from Aditya Chakrabortty's piece in *The Guardian*, reflecting on the lowered economic growth seen in the UK in the aftermath of the referendum:

> There's a lady I've been thinking about for the past few days, even though we've never met. She's the central character in a true story told by the Europe expert Anand

Menon. He was in Newcastle just before the referendum to debate the impact of Britain leaving the EU. Invoking the gods of economics, the King's College London professor invited the audience to imagine the likely plunge in the UK's GDP. Back yelled the woman: 'That's your bloody GDP. Not ours.'[21]

In that single howl, so much is summed up. Every time I have used that phrase to senior business executives throughout the whole Brexit drama they have stopped in their tracks. In a sentence it brought to life why the economic argument alone didn't work. Those cold economic facts that seemed to be winning the day for most business executives in 2016 were not enough to win the wider democratic argument in the end. The idea that 'the few' had benefited from globalisation, digital progress and zero hours working was palpable among voters. Most business leaders didn't understand it.

Christian May, the zesty editor of *City AM*, is a good friend. We voted in different directions on Brexit, but his analysis for this book is something I share here: 'I don't think business has been stunned by the political class over the last few years. I think it has been stunned by coming into contact with the electorate, which it often goes out of its way to avoid.'

This idea is felt by others. Dame Helena Morrissey, the City fund manager who defines herself away from the herd and is now with Legal & General, was one of the few major City voices to publicly back Brexit. She told me:

---

21 Aditya Chakrabortty, 'One blunt heckler has revealed just how much the UK economy is failing us', *The Guardian*, 10 January 2017.

I remember being at one of those City grandee roundtables in 2016 and the insightful pollster Deborah Mattinson [Gordon Brown's chief polling guru] had placed on the table some compelling voter research which showed there was a huge lack of trust in the City and the wider business sector since the financial crisis and that its message was not landing. The response from the group was to turn up the volume not to change the message. It was at that point that I knew Vote Leave could win.

Morrissey says there was such a lack of awareness among business figures about how voters outside the bubble of Westminster and the City were feeling. 'There was a brief period after the financial crash when there was some realism – but it didn't last very long and we went back to business as usual,' she points out. Another senior BBC editorial figure put it to me a different way. Katy Searle is head of BBC Westminster. She told me: 'It comes down to trust. The financial crash meant that voters no longer trusted the "clever people" to protect their interests. There has been a huge collapse in trust and the belief that the establishment may not know best after all.'

It was this insight that led Theresa May – and her closest advisers Nick Timothy and Fiona Hill – to ensure that in the first year of her premiership, business would be seen to be firmly locked out of decisions on Brexit. It would be excluded from meaningful conversations about the strategy and it would be attacked as corporatist, global and out of touch. In pure political terms it might have appeared to be the right approach to show to voters there would be a step change from the Cameron cosiness with the corporatists, but it was to prove fatal for trust between politics and business. Juergen Maier, the Siemens UK CEO, told me: 'Reflecting on the entire period I don't think the relationship between business and politics has been this low since the mid-1970s.'

The Prime Minister had also spent months telling the electorate and business that there would not be an early general election. When that fact changed, famously Brenda from Bristol caught the mood of a nation when she uttered: 'Not another one!' in a BBC news video that went viral – but remarkably she also spoke for a business class now exhausted by the continued festival of democracy which had started to resemble a relentless US electoral cycle with major polls being held every two years. Rather than getting on with decision making with a secure majority, the Prime Minister took a calculated gamble on going to the country to get her own mandate.

Like everyone else, I was caught on the hop. I had travelled to China in April 2017 to understand more about the country and its ambitions. I was there at the time of the latest Belt and Road conference, a biannual event which looks to bring more and more Western involvement and investment into the monumental initiative to create a seamless infrastructure superhighway from Europe to the East. The word 'awesome' is overused, but in this case it is just that. An awe-inspiring political and economic ambition without parallel. Of course, the project raises a wider debate about Chinese economic intentions, but this is not the place to explore that. Many UK firms had been looking to get involved but in the first few months of 2017 there was no UK political space for such conversations or British involvement.

In the midst of my trip on 18 April 2017 I was sitting in the vast Beijing International Airport about to board a flight to Seoul for a short break. I had never been to Korea before but – like China – the scale of the political and economic partnership with business has actually delivered economic prosperity for millions. I visited the excellent Seoul Museum of History, which tells the story of the country's economic and social journey before and since the brutal Korean War. It has a whole section on how business has been the driver of economic prosperity in the south since the 1960s. The sense that personal GDP is linked to the growing macroeconomic story of that country is palpable. While the relationship between Korea's major corporations and Korean politicians can be aptly described as 'cosy' and 'corporatist' – and there have been evident scandals as a result of that cosiness – there is an overall sense of business and politics working together for an economic prize that works across South Korean society. It was good to reflect on that at least. Just before I boarded the plane, my assistant Kerensa Grant texted me on my China secure mobile phone. 'I think you had better look at the news – it looks like Theresa May is about to call a general election,' she said. Sure enough, it was confirmed shortly after. A seven-week campaign was ahead of us – but at least I would have a few days in Korea to charge the batteries for the political madness ahead, I thought.

The plane ride back to London provided me with the opportunity to digest that pro-business Korean culture and capture some ideas. Was the idea of such an economic partnership ever possible in the UK, I wondered? It also provided me with the chance to catch up on the first week of this unexpected UK election. The Prime Minister's massive 21-point polling lead would have tempted any political leader to head to the country. The fact that Article 50 had been invoked was also a strong signal to the electorate and to her party that she was already delivering on Brexit. I wrote one of my analysis notes for clients over a glass of wine as we flew back over China. It was probably a combination of the altitude and the flowing British Airways pinot noir, but I succumbed to the seduction of those polling numbers. It was clear to the pollsters that Theresa May would be back in Downing Street with an enhanced super-majority, and that majority was likely to strengthen the rhetoric against Brussels. That is what I told business. Despite what her policy chief John Godfrey had told me about the Prime Minister's intentions, I warned business to be ready for a further influx of Eurosceptics onto the Tory benches and a stiffening of UK political resolve.

But within hours of landing back in the UK I sensed a very different mood in my interactions with those inside the Tory election campaign. The narrative of the election had been built around the personality of the Prime Minister herself. On the most important issue for business – Brexit and the economy – you could barely hear a word from the Chancellor Philip Hammond. This was, of course, a deliberate strategy from those at the heart of the campaign. Voters would be asked to focus their attention on Theresa May and not the rest of her Cabinet. This would give her maximum authority when she won and it was presumed her Chancellor would be despatched to the back benches shortly after. Most businesspeople looked on in horror. Hammond had been one of the key voices around the Cabinet table consistently arguing for a soft economic landing from Brexit, a transition and a deal.

But making this campaign centre around Theresa May was of course its undoing. I remember sitting at home watching Andrew Neil surgically take apart the Conservative manifesto in an interview with Theresa May on 22 May 2017, thinking that the Tory campaign was coming off the rails. As a communications man, I still shudder when I think of that interview. With all the trappings of her office, this was perhaps the worst political interview from a Prime Minister in a generation.

Craig Oliver – of course no cheerleader for Theresa May, either while working for David Cameron in No. 10 or since – told me for this book:

> They built a strategy on the belief that a 24-point lead and a few focus groups would see them through. That was it. But the combination of a robotic leader at the centre of a Presidential-style campaign and a toxic manifesto did for them. In truth, anyone in their circumstances would probably have gone for it – but it's a cautionary tale about hubris, lack of self-knowledge and how volatile British politics is.

And Oliver was right. In my analysis at the time for businesses I noted that Theresa May had been introduced to the British electorate on only four occasions since she became Prime Minister. The first time was her speech on the steps of Downing Street on 13 July 2016 when she talked of the 'burning injustices' in British society. The second speech was her party conference address in October 2016 where she had labelled many businesspeople as 'citizens of nowhere'. The third was the Lancaster House speech of January 2017 where she laid out her red lines on the EU. And finally, in April 2017, when she stood outside Downing Street again and called the general election itself.

While there had been countless Prime Minister's Questions appearances where she had regularly bested Jeremy Corbyn, there was no regular 'look down the lens' moment with the public or 'town halls' with voters, which David Cameron and Tony Blair had used to great effect. Of course, as the campaign unfolded, we would come to understand why. The short-circuited Tory leadership campaign had served Theresa May well. It still amazes me that an essentially extremely private person like Theresa May can make it to the top in the modern era of 24-hour news. But Gordon Brown faced his own demons with the media, and many other world leaders have a similar shyness and inability to wear their hearts on their sleeves. It's a strange trait for professional politicians, but I have found it to be more common than you'd think.

Beyond the Prime Minister's campaign performance, it was the Tory manifesto itself that was to prove to be so disastrous. Its centrepiece was a plan to tackle one of those burning injustices: the failing social care system for older people across the country. In my work with the insurance sector, the policy debate on social care had been a huge part of my lobbying under the two previous governments. Andy Burnham as the Labour Health Secretary under Gordon Brown had set off a national debate on social care, but trying to forge a cross-party consensus on the issue had proved futile. It was a prime example where politicians were unwilling or just attitudinally unable to work together and come to a common solution. Just a few years earlier the Blair government had forged a generation-lasting consensus on auto-enrolment into workplace pensions, but social care seemed to mire in much more partisan politics. It had been a foretaste of things to come.

When the coalition was formed in 2010 the Conservatives and the Lib Dems had to work to bury their differences and come together. The then government commissioned the respected economist Andrew Dilnot within weeks of taking office to launch a Commission on Social Care. It reported one year later in July 2011. It proposed urgent reforms, including a more generous means-testing threshold to support care, a cap on care costs, the need to incorporate complex disability benefits and a reduction in the postcode lottery for care services. The insurance sector and international investors saw a big opportunity to get involved and be partners in a massive scale-up of care services to provide coverage for millions of people. But, despite these detailed and workable plans, the coalition could not get in place a sustainable underpinning from taxpayers to make this work. The big focus at the Department for Work and Pensions was rolling out the plans for Iain Duncan Smith's Universal Credit plan. Needless to say, Universal Credit might best be described as being like Brexit for the DWP for the entire duration of the coalition government: it swamped the department and its Secretary of State. Nothing else really got a look in at the Cabinet table.

Before the coalition left office in spring 2015, some small aspects of the Care Act came into force, but there was much left to do. An opportunity to solve the problem for the long term had been missed by Cameron and Clegg and there was huge disappointment. Beyond that, the costs for local authorities – already stretched by austerity – were coming into sharp relief. By the spring of 2017, the social care problem had become a big issue among Tory voters. The Conservative-controlled Local Government Association (LGA) was becoming increasingly vocal and had success-fully wound up the *Daily Mail*, who, by the end of 2016, was running a campaign that was making waves. Indeed, in December 2016, the *Mail* spurred its campaign further with a front-page headline titled 'Put Our Needy Elderly First!', criticising the proposed rise in council tax to fund social care provision (instead arguing for a reduction in the foreign aid budget). As part of our work at Cicero, I had pointed the insurance sector towards the campaign to pump up the volume for policy action. After years of inactivity from poli-cymakers, the media- and LGA-led activity was working and there was clearly an opportunity to secure reform. The LGA had started to say – in advance of crucial local elections – that council taxes would be rising to pay for increasing social care costs. So, the LGA was attacking its own government head-on with an argument that called for directly hypoth-ecated (or linked) council taxes to pay for the increasing social care needs. For many in Westminster I could hear the oft-chimed mantra: 'These are our voters – something must be done.'

I had witnessed the problem myself. My elderly parents

lived in the Scottish countryside at the time. While the Scottish social care system was supposedly much better, we had found it almost impossible to get care support that worked for the carers and for my parents.

In February 2017, I had one of my regular check-in meetings with No. 10 policy chief John Godfrey back in Downing Street. He told me: 'We are working on paying for social care as the centrepiece of the domestic policy agenda. If we can crack this, this will be the keynote reform of the May era outside delivering Brexit.' He asked me for support from the insurance sector with ideas. He had been working with the then Cabinet Office minister Ben Gummer on a comprehensive agenda – but when it came to the Tories' election manifesto in spring 2017, it appears all this work was barely given a sideways glance by Nick Timothy, who held the pen on the document himself. Written in highly secretive circumstances with little input from the wider Cabinet and from those – like Godfrey – who had been engaged deep in the weeds of the complex technical and fiscal issues around care reform for years before he entered government, the soundbite policy on social care that appeared in the manifesto bore little relation to the hard work and analysis of Dilnot, Godfrey and the insurance industry.

On the morning of 18 May 2017, when the Tories revealed their manifesto, Dilnot killed the central idea of the Tory plan stone dead with a devastating interview on the *Today* programme, hours before it was formally launched. The Tory manifesto had removed the cap on care costs, which Dilnot said would leave people 'helpless'. He told the *Today* programme:

There's nothing you can do to protect yourself against care costs, you can't insure it because the private sector won't insure it, and by refusing to implement the cap [on costs] the Conservatives are now saying that they are not going to provide social insurance for it either ... People will be left helpless knowing that what will happen is if they're unlucky enough to suffer the need for care costs, they'll be entirely on their own ... The analogy is a bit like saying to somebody, you can't insure your house against burning down, if it does burn down then you are completely on your own.

The centre of the Tory manifesto was quickly dubbed the 'dementia tax'. Over three days of campaigning during the intense weekend of 19–21 May, Tory canvassers heard the words 'dementia tax' more than ever in a blast of icy air from their own voters on the doorstep. Many of those voters – as had been correctly identified by the LGA earlier that year – had 'done the right thing' and saved for their retirement. By 22 May, the Prime Minister was telling the media that 'nothing has changed', despite the fact that the manifesto policy had been dropped, the cap had been reinstated and the big 'domestic idea' for the manifesto was consigned to the political bin.

Within weeks of the election I was sitting with new Work and Pensions Secretary David Gauke in his Whitehall office talking about the need to not lose the political moment and press ahead with reforming social care. Surely this would be part of the legacy of the government with its agenda of social reform. I told him that while the election debate had gone wrong, they had the opportunity to make amends as millions of voters had just focused on the subject for the first time. I said there remained an appetite from the insurance sector to help deliver a credible solution if the government would step up too. Gauke told me with a sigh: 'We want to deliver on this, but the politics now makes it so difficult.' The good thing was the Tory manifesto highlighted the problem. The tragedy for the country (and for my own parents and indeed millions of others) is that three years on – to use a current political maxim – nothing has changed.

The wider disaster was unfolding for Theresa May in the election. Corbyn was powering his campaign and performing better on the election stage than anyone had predicted. My Labour-leaning Cicero colleagues were not surprised. Tom Frackowiak, our UK public policy director, told me at the time: 'Remember, Corbyn is a highly effective campaigner – he always has been. This is his preferred territory.' Corbyn's message, which focused on the economy, was hitting home. He talked about the 'few' who have benefited from globalisation and the digitisation of the economy, and it struck a chord. As anti-business as ever, the sentiments chimed.

During the campaign, a young technology guru who had been working to support Lord Ashcroft's polling operation came to see me and Cicero's research director Mark Twigg at our London offices. He was hoping to promote his 'micro-targeting' approach to our clients to allow them to better understand voter trends. He proudly opened his laptop and presented data on the likely Tory election tsunami ahead. Neither Mark nor I were so sure, and when he opened the page on the likely results from the Rother Valley and predicted a Tory majority of around 750, Mark could barely contain himself. Hailing from Rotherham, Mark told the pollster: 'These numbers are utter rubbish. I can tell you now that the Rother Valley is not about to elect a Tory MP.' The meeting abruptly ended. But Labour's Kevin Barron was returned to Westminster as the Member of Parliament for Rother Valley with a massively reduced majority of 3,882. Therefore, the trend had been right when the young pollster presented it, but the Tory strategy had simply failed to work, as there was a huge swing back to Labour in the final two weeks of the election.

On the night of the general election, Cicero was the lead sponsor for the Institute of Directors election night party in the grand surroundings of their Pall Mall headquarters in London's club land. This was a prime opportunity for my business to project its brand to the key business community interested in being with and around policymakers. As every-one arrived mid-evening to grab a pre-results drink, all the chatter was about the size of the Tory majority. Guests had even placed their bets on such an outcome. Before the 10 p.m. unveiling of the all-important exit polls I had taken numerous calls from international investors, as always in such events. On nights like these our team at Cicero will send the latest data and analysis to business far and wide including many in the UK, Wall Street and Asia. Before the polls closed the consensus was clear. The Tories would win and May – while not set for a super-majority – would probably en-hance Cameron's result and have approximately a sixty-seat advantage.

Christian May and I debated the likely trajectory ahead

with the IoD's then chief lobbyist Andy Silvester in front of a packed room of 600 business leaders. We all thought the same. So, at 10 p.m., when David Dimbleby unveiled on the BBC election night programme that Britain was set to have a hung parliament, you could hear the oxygen leave the room instantly. John Godfrey – who I had watched and met with often across the first year of the Theresa May government – downed an entire glass of red wine in one gulp and promptly left the party.

Andy Silvester and I went back on stage and predicted the imminent demise of Theresa May. Christian May ran back to his newsroom to rewrite his front page. But instantly business turned towards the likelihood of a much more difficult trajectory for May's Brexit plans. Almost everyone thought this would point towards a softer Brexit as Parliament would be likely to block any attempt to take the UK out of the EU without a deal, but all were aware that the Brexit clock was ticking. All the election had done was confuse business even more and make the horizon even more cloudy – and to waste valuable negotiating time. But as Nick Timothy and Fiona Hill were swept out of Downing Street in the wee small hours following the election, one person seemed much more secure in his seat – Chancellor Philip Hammond. Predicted to be booted out of No. 11 after a huge May win, Hammond would prove to have staying power. For business, his voice at the table was to prove crucial in the months and years ahead.

The regular weekly meeting was held between business groups and Greg Clark the morning after the election. Clark had hosted these meetings almost every week since he became Business Secretary. The mood was basically one of baffled shock, once again, not exactly helped by the fact that half of the room had been watching the election until the early hours. Clark was trying to manoeuvre the business groups towards a softer Brexit and unite them behind a single plan. However, a few hours later the meeting leaked to the *Financial Times*. One who was present at the meeting told me: 'In theory Clark was livid. I say in theory because to this day I am convinced that the leak came from his own department.'

Summing up my feelings for business and finance, I took to print in the financial title *Money Marketing* the week after the election: 'What a mess. There are no other words for it. An election that was supposed to produce a strong and stable government has produced a weak and wobbly one.'

9

THE REGULATORS AWAKE

The day after the election night before was not a glad, happy morning for anyone. Not for the Prime Minister, nor Britain's businesses. The country appeared to be all at sea and, just one year on from the Brexit referendum, political watchers had been caught on the hop once again. The expected result – a government with a very healthy majority – had not transpired and the certainty that all business craves had turned to dust. I spent another very long day trying to decipher Britain's political mess for domestic and international businesses. Many of them had seen the mess coming before the political pollsters and had started to trade against the currency during the campaign. In fact, I often think that political watchers would do better to 'follow the money' rather than the psephological machinations of the polling companies who – rather reliably these days – keep getting their macro predictions wrong while accurately predicting final polling numbers with a 3 per cent margin of error.

On 9 June 2017, the DUP website crashed as mainstream political analysis shifted to pore over the DUP manifesto. Northern Ireland's main party offered Theresa May the only possible mathematical way out of the mess. But involvement of the DUP in any political permutation ahead also pointed towards a harder Brexit outcome. The DUP had backed Leave despite the referendum result in Northern Ireland back in June 2016 which had marginally backed Remain. A longstanding Euroscepticism in the DUP was always governed by what this meant for the position of Northern Ireland in the UK. Businesses with a large presence in Northern Ireland, especially the banks, started dusting off their DUP contact books and talking in earnest to the most important Westminster party after the Conservatives.

There was a strange echo of what had happened between 2015 and 2017, when the SNP surge and Lib Dem collapse changed British politics. For those two years the SNP was often more effective in playing the role of the opposition than the Labour Party. Labour MPs were riven by the election of Jeremy Corbyn, who faced another leadership challenge from Owen Smith immediately after the Brexit referendum in 2016. Business saw in the SNP a more united and coherent approach towards opposition and often beat a path to the SNP's door. The contrast was striking. For years Alex Salmond had hoovered up 'tartan Tory' votes and, in contrast to the state ownership ambitions of the Labour Party, the SNP seemed both moderate and business-friendly. According to Salmond's former chief of staff Geoff Aberdein:

> There was a huge outreach to business during Alex's [Salmond] leadership. Business had also got to know the SNP well in advance of the independence referendum and there was a very open dialogue. Of course, many business

leaders did not want to support independence but a dialogue had been established. Doors were open.

There was a brief attempt by business to get to know the DUP in the same way after the June 2017 election, but it never really caught the imagination of either side in the same way that the SNP dialogue had done. More than that, the DUP business agenda on Brexit was in the wrong place for most enterprises. Put simply, there was not a lot to talk about.

Within days, we could see another impact of the election. The door had occasionally been open in the first year of the May regime, but the rhetoric had been so hardcore. Business felt shut out. Following the election, the mood changed almost overnight. With her former chiefs of staff leaving the building, there was a shift in gear and a recognition that business needed to be listened to again and that government needed to show that publicly and privately. As one long-term No. 10 insider put it to me for this book: 'There was a feeling that under the Cameron–Osborne era there had been a revolving door and access was very easy for the biggest businesses. It is not that the PM, or indeed Nick Timothy or former lobbyist Fiona Hill, were anti-business – if anything they were anti-corporatist.'

Leading the business relations team at No. 10 for the first year of the May government was Chris Brannigan. Brannigan had served in the army and seen service in Iraq and Afghanistan, and he had brought his operational skills into politics as part of the Conservative Party's management team under Cameron's leadership. May's team brought him into Downing Street to work on business relations. It was to prove to be a thankless task and he quickly left the No. 10 machine demoralised from the experience following the election in 2017.

Brannigan had spent a tortuous year at the heart of government trying to keep the door open when the rhetoric from the Prime Minister kept slamming it in the faces of British business. Not long after he left No. 10 in the summer of 2017, he came to see me at Cicero. There was no doubt he was pleased to have left, saying: 'I spent a whole year at the heart of government and I am unable to tell you what the Prime Minister actually thinks about business.' He had also lifted the lid on the personality of the Prime Minister when dealing with business leaders, which provided an insight into her psyche which I had guessed but did not know until that moment. He told me: 'I spent my time briefing business leaders before they met the PM in some detail. I told them the Prime Minister would not make the first move in any conversation. You will have to do all the talking.' This was absolutely the case. On briefing senior business leaders before they were going to meet the Prime Minister, I would tell them to come armed with a range of detailed policy asks alongside an armoury of small talk to keep the conversation flowing.

When Cicero launched its business in Ireland in the early part of 2018, I heard from numerous sources that one of the reasons why Theresa May and Irish Taoiseach Leo Varadkar had such a poor interpersonal relationship was because neither of them do small talk. Varadkar's predecessor Enda Kenny was a master of the 'blarney' and could put anyone at ease, which he did with May. But Varadkar was different.

He is like May in many ways, but most notably they are both incredibly shy. In fact, government officials on both the UK and Ireland side of negotiations created a whole set of small-talk ideas to get the conversation started between the two leaders. In so many ways this insight reflects the reasons why the relationship – or lack of it – between the leaders added to the Brexit negotiating crisis and made the talks about the Irish border situation even worse. I have often reflected that modern politics – which is built on the soundbite – has created such an artificial way of talking that our political leaders are not as good at speaking to each other any more. It is perhaps much of the reason for the negotiating quagmire that we have been in.

From the summer of 2017, there was a distinct attempt to bring business back into No. 10 and to improve the dialogue with government. Rather than political micromanagement from the chiefs of staff, I also got the sense that the Cabinet Office and the machinery of government were more firmly in control of things. At the Treasury, because Philip Hammond remained in his seat, and while Greg Clark remained at BEIS, the government suddenly appeared to be more open to business and its Brexit concerns. Nevertheless, its Brexit 'strategy' was not evident to most of us engaging with it. The nods and winks we had received in the previous year to expect a 'soft' outcome were not being made evident in the political rhetoric, which was designed to keep the hard Brexiteers onside in Parliament for as long as possible in the negotiations. But within weeks of the 2017 general election, three things happened to make business feel that it was really being listened to and that there was a shape of a plan.

The first thing was the reshaping of the government itself. Some new ministers were in place who wanted to take the time to listen to business. For finance, it was a relief to have a new City minister. Simon Kirby, who had been in the role until the general election and had not covered himself in glory, lost his Brighton Kemptown seat in the early hours of 9 June. The formation of the new government, with the DUP, was to take several weeks, and it was not until 14 June that the new Economic Secretary (the formal title of the City minister) would be in place at the Treasury. Steve Barclay, MP for North East Cambridgeshire and a government whip, was catapulted into the front line for the first time.

I had known Steve for over a decade. Before entering Parliament in 2010, he had worked in senior roles at Barclays and latterly at the Financial Conduct Authority. We had worked briefly together and I had provided him with ideas for the think tank the Centre for Policy Studies, who had produced a pamphlet back in 2005 entitled 'The Leviathan is still at large'. This was a collaborative effort to provide a context for reform to the UK's financial regulatory structure, which many of us believed needed further reform. It was written before the financial crisis started to unfold in 2007, but many of its recommendations found their way into government – specifically, that the UK regulators needed to become more 'pro-consumer competition' in their mandate and in their policies. The work provided George Osborne with the basis for the reform of the tripartite Bank of England–Financial Conduct Authority–HM Treasury structure which had overseen the financial crisis. The new Financial

Conduct Authority set up by Osborne would be even more pro-competition than its predecessor.

Barclay and I agreed on the approach towards many things, but we had been on opposite sides of the fence on Brexit. For him it was a matter of principle and practicality, and his constituency would vote 69.4 per cent to leave the EU. (As we have seen since the referendum, it would always be easier for an MP to be in lockstep with the vast majority of their constituents.) Nevertheless, given our relationship I wanted to reach out to Barclay to help him in the early days of his new role. We met together for a 7 a.m. breakfast in London's Soho in early July 2017 and I briefed him – with no officials present – on the state of mind of the financial services sector. Barclay told me we needed to meet so early because his ministerial diary was already being packed out each day from 8 a.m. by his officials. Specifically, I told him about the Simon Kirby car crash in front of TheCityUK grandees back in November 2016. At this stage Barclay seemed totally unaware of those events. Officials had clearly been kind to his predecessor, but I knew they were as pleased as me to have a minister eager to shine in the role and work hard to do so.

I told him: 'Steve – most businesses are feeling very locked out of decision making right now. Worse than that, there is a sense that government is not taking their views seriously. I urge you to use your position to reach out and be seen to listen and take action.'

To quickly address concerns, I asked him to come and address TheCityUK's next Advisory Committee meeting later in July, the same group Kirby had met in 2016. I said to him:

'Come and talk to them. Make clear you are in listening mode. Spend more time listening than talking. Don't do the usual thing which ministers do which is to speak at length and then hastily leave the room. Stay. Exhaust their questions. They won't expect you to know all the answers at this stage. If you don't know the answer promise to write back to them.'

A few days later TheCityUK grandees gathered in Canary Wharf at the offices of EY, hosted by their forward-thinking financial sector lead Omar Ali. Omar and I have spent much of our time since the Brexit referendum working with the same financial sector businesses helping them to navigate the headwinds. My job is different to his; he focuses on helping businesses to do the rewiring they need to secure market access. He had become a real friend over the past few years as we have shared this difficult journey together. We are both outsiders to the City 'establishment' and have built our careers precisely by challenging it.

Barclay addressed the meeting and was pitch perfect. He spoke briefly, and he exhausted the grandees and their questions. When he left the room, the immediate reaction was clear. The new City minister cared about the City and was not craven. He was a realist and he had the intellectual heft to take on board complex issues. He was good news. I texted Barclay from inside the meeting as he travelled back in the ministerial Toyota Prius with his officials to Whitehall. 'You smashed it. Well done.' Almost as soon as Barclay had left the room, the then chair of the Financial Conduct Authority, John Griffith-Jones, addressed the gathering. He too had been impressed by Barclay and confirmed the regulator had seen a marked uptick in energy and engagement from the new minister. He also expressed his frustrations with the current Brexit process and told the room: 'We are in deep dialogue with the regulators across the EU and the relations privately remain very good. If the politicians weren't running the process, I think we could get to an agreement for financial services really quickly.'

Speaking to me for this book, the CEO of the Financial Conduct Authority, Andrew Bailey, told me:

The financial crisis meant that we were more prepared for Brexit. We have had several key principles governing our approach. Firstly, that regulation would be up and running on day one after Brexit. That there would be continuity. Secondly that systemic risk would be addressed. Thirdly that our guiding principle would be 'open' markets.

Former German CDU MEP Burkhard Balz, who is now a director of the Bundesbank (the German central regulator), went on: 'The UK will look to its advantages and that will be the case with its regulatory regime.'

Of course, Brexit has been a political process. If the economics had trumped the politics then the result might have been very different. But it was reassuring to know – at that stage at least – that the regulators were on the case. As we moved into 2018 and 2019, it would be harder and harder for the EU regulators to agree to anything as their political masters in Brussels held them back. That paralysis was to send many finance chiefs crazy and make them do the only thing they could to secure their future business: plan to beef up their operations inside the EU.

However, Griffith-Jones pointed to the next stages of the drama for finance. The regulators – led by the Bank of England and the Prudential Regulation Authority (PRA) – would now be writing to all the major banking, insurance and asset management firms to ask them to provide their detailed plans to ensure there was going to be no systemic disruption to the financial system from a hard Brexit. The PRA had been part of George Osborne's grand plan to ensure that the UK regulators would learn the lessons of the 2008 financial crash and to get ahead of any future financial shocks to the economy by focusing on prudential regulation – that is, system-wide oversight of finance to make sure economic bubbles don't burst or the financial plumbing that holds together modern economics doesn't leak. Over the summer of 2017, the PRA wrote to the major financial firms with a simple ask: 'Show us your plans and we will rate their effectiveness.'

Over the next year and into the autumn of 2018, the firms responded, with many of them having to rewrite their thinking fundamentally. I will look later at how business used the autumn of 2017 and spring of 2018 to make their final decisions on where to locate.

'When we look back, we will owe a huge debt of gratitude to the UK regulators for navigating Brexit so effectively for the City,' Christian May told me. 'I think Mark Carney and Andrew Bailey, in particular, have been excellent all the way through the difficult politics.' While Inga Beale, Lloyds of London CEO through most of the negotiations, told me: 'Our regulators have been running the show and they have helped us greatly.' But she also reflected on some of the more 'cosmetic' engagement that the May government offered with business. Her concern was that the government was holding countless meetings but essentially always asking the same questions.

In the summers of 2017 and 2018, the Brexit Secretaries of the time – David Davis and his successor, Dominic Raab – organised business summits at the Foreign Secretary's grace and favour country mansion, Chevening House. A range of FTSE businesses and inward investors were invited to attend alongside the big and small business bodies – the IoD, CBI and the FSB. Rather than offering an opportunity for meaningful dialogue, the business leaders were treated to speeches from ministers and presentations which told them nothing new. According to Inga Beale: 'The Chevening meetings with Davis and Raab felt like we were just going through the motions and not being seriously listened to.'

What was the effect of all this? The regulators in the UK and the EU were more confident that firms who had used London as their passport into the EU now had plans to ensure that there would be no business disruption for markets and for their customers. As a result, EU regulators could see firms relocating into their zone and therefore had less and less of an incentive to make life easy for firms based in the UK, so they would not take decisions to undermine the Brussels negotiating hand. Further, those businesses themselves started to become more and more relaxed about the eventual outcome. Whatever the UK government might do, and whatever the EU27 might do, they had a plan. Of course there was a wider political impact taking place in

Westminster itself. The 2015 parliament was cut short, and some MPs had decided to call it a day. One of them was Treasury Select Committee (TSC) chair Andrew Tyrie MP. Tyrie had taken the mantle on in 2010, succeeding Labour's John McFall. The chair is always, by convention, filled by someone from the governing party. During his tenure chairing the committee, McFall had developed a fearsome reputation for calling the masters of finance to account. CEOs had been destroyed by their inability to master the politics of the TSC and had been rapidly despatched thereafter. So much so that when Andrew Tyrie ascended to chair the committee in 2010, the standard journalistic formula to describe the TSC was 'all-powerful'.

When I spoke to McFall just before he left the House of Commons in 2010, he told me: 'My committee must have been very good for your business. We had the masters of finance quaking in their shoes and we brought about huge change in the debate.' He was spot on. Tyrie was to cut a very different kind of figure in the chair but had McFall's legacy to turn to. While McFall was great at creating change by mastering the theatre of the TSC cockpit to generate front-page news, Tyrie would use forensic questioning to catch his fish.

One of my colleagues at Cicero holds the record for the longest lobbying meeting with any MP. He spent almost four hours incarcerated in Tyrie's office on the parliamentary estate in the old Norman Shaw buildings, which had – rather ironically – previously housed Scotland Yard. The only break in the meeting was when Tyrie and the client wanted to go for a cigarette. It was Tyrie's style – he was interested in the depth of the argument and stayed as far away from soundbite populism as it was possible for a politician to be by the mid-2010s.

A new system had been put in place following the 2010 election to elect the chairs of the Select Committees by a vote of all MPs, to replace the 'smoke-filled stitch-up' between the party whips. In the ballot to become the new TSC chair in 2017 there were two front runners. Nicky Morgan MP, a Remain supporter in the referendum who had been Cameron's Education Secretary and was a highly successful City minister before then, was pitched against Jacob Rees-Mogg MP, who went on to chair the European Research Group (ERG) and was a City fund manager and backer of the Leave cause. It was to be a parliamentary version of the Brexit referendum itself for the right to lead one of its most important bodies.

Morgan and Rees-Mogg ran very different campaigns. Morgan's pitch was to hold the government to account on the delivery of Brexit and to ensure the regulators would do all they could to support a soft landing for the finance sector. Rees-Mogg – already in a war of words with Bank of England Governor Mark Carney over his macroeconomic predictions during the Brexit referendum – wanted to ask a very different question. To paraphrase: 'Are the regulators forcing businesses out of Britain?'

Morgan won the MPs' vote with a healthy majority and set about using the agenda of the committee to achieve a soft Brexit. She also pushed the regulators hard on the question of ensuring that UK finance would have access to the single market. As one of the biggest proponents for a Norway-style deal with the EU, Morgan wanted to see – like the regulators themselves – no cliff-edge or systemic disruption. But she also had a wider ambition. When we spoke ahead of this book, she said: 'I have seen the role of the Treasury Select Committee – particularly when business was not even being invited into government – as a platform to give business a voice in the heart of Parliament.'

There is no doubt that Morgan took that role seriously. Indeed, upon her election as chair of the committee, Morgan called for the financial services industry to be given greater clarity regarding the government's Brexit plans and criticised the fact that ministers had not yet published a position paper on Brexit and financial services.[22]

So with a fresh set of ministers in place, regulators who were working as hard as possible to make sure there were no economic ill-effects and a Treasury Select Committee determined to ask the right questions to support those efforts, many businesses felt more confident about those steering the ship in the wake of the 2017 snap election. But – and it was an important but – businesses still believed that they needed to prepare for the worst.

It seemed to me that large businesses were increasingly sorting their Brexit strategies; smaller ones had their fingers crossed behind their backs.

22 'UK government under fire for leaving finance sector in dark on Brexit', Reuters, 22 January 2018.

10

GETTING ON WITH IT

If business needed a wake-up call to start preparing for a chaotic Brexit process, the 2017 election had provided just that. Alongside the UK regulators' assertive push to ensure our economy would be able to function throughout the negotiations and out of the EU, firms had long since moved out of the 'emotional' phase and had resorted to their usual mindset. Rational and coldly economic, business was now starting to spend on Brexit mitigation in earnest. That was indeed the mindset for most business I could see. The sunlit uplands of any 'new world' outside the EU would be years away for most. The immediate priority was to secure market access with the biggest trading bloc right on our doorstep. This wasn't political at all – it was just good business.

At Cicero, we had seen our business grow over 20 per cent by the end of 2016, despite the concerns of the effect that the referendum result might have upon us, as it became clear there was a huge appetite for political risk analysis. Uncertainty, sadly, was rather good for business. I had never seen a period like it. Brexit was perhaps the biggest planned political risk event for most large businesses. At the same time, my friends in the big management consultancies and 'magic circle' global law firms told me they were not immediately able to monetise the Brexit effect. By the end of 2016, most of them had launched their Brexit services to clients but they all told me that there was no money to be made as most business remained paralysed by their inability to decide on what to do.

However, by the summer of 2017 things were very different and I could see that colleagues in the major firms including EY, Deloitte and KPMG, as well as the big City law firms like Clifford Chance, Freshfields and Hogan Lovells, were starting to work on major restructuring projects for the City. The promises – some called them empty threats – made during the referendum to locate business into the EU area were starting to take place. Omar Ali, lead financial services partner at EY, told me:

> By the summer of 2017, doing nothing was not an option any more for most of the global financial firms who had used London as their passporting route into the EU. With so much uncertainty around they needed to start work on rewiring their businesses to make sure they could safeguard market access and to satisfy their regulators in time.

By spring 2019, EY calculated that around £1 trillion in assets being managed out of London's financial centre had been moved into the EU in time for a potential 29 March cliff-edge.[23]

On 19 October 2017, Lloyd Blankfein, CEO of Goldman Sachs and one of Wall Street's best-known financiers, took to

---

23 'EY Financial Services Tracker: Financial Services firms put contingency plans in action as asset and job relocation continues to increase', EY, 20 March 2019.

Twitter: 'Just left Frankfurt. Great meetings, great weather, really enjoyed it. Good, because I'll be spending a lot more time there. #Brexit.' While the UK tabloids and the shrillest of Brexiteers screamed 'good riddance', those more concerned with keeping together the City of London felt very despondent. Money was already moving, and some key jobs and functions too. It appeared our politicians and our businesses were shouting at each other.

My visits to Dublin in 2016 and other key locations inside the EU were beginning to pay dividends for my business. At Cicero we had established a network of connections with policymakers and regulators across the EU that would prove critical for firms looking for intelligence on their location options to secure ongoing passporting rights. My team now had a detailed roadmap on the likely political and regulatory 'welcome' any business might be given in Ireland, Poland, Holland, Luxembourg, Germany, Italy and France. Over the months ahead, clients would lean heavily on this resource as they developed their detailed restructuring plans with their lawyers and the management consultants.

Days after the disastrous general election, on 19 June 2017, David Davis went to Brussels and started the UK negotiations with EU Brexit chief negotiator Michel Barnier. The UK government had indicated that it wanted to undertake a 'concurrent' negotiation, which would involve making a deal on the new trade relationship at the same time as negotiating the divorce arrangements. However, on day one the UK abandoned attempts to force the EU to start talks on trade; instead, its 'exit bill' would be the starting point for the talks. The hard man approach from Davis had crumbled immediately. My analysis for business was that the EU would continue to have the upper hand in the negotiations all the way to the finish line, but most businesses knew that and were working accordingly. That the UK caved in was a recognition of the fact that it had not bottomed out its own negotiating position, either in government or, fatefully, across Parliament, before starting to negotiate with Brussels. Without UK Cabinet agreement on a single approach towards the negotiations, the problems were storing up ahead.

Nevertheless, one policy benefit for business emerged from the UK government's stance. For all of 2016 and through the election campaign there had been a real concern that EU citizens living and working in the EU would be used as bargaining chips in the negotiations. This had been governed by the Prime Minister's own political narrative around freedom of movement, which she had honed as Home Secretary into her own political brand, and it had driven some of the most prominent Brexiteers, like Jacob Rees-Mogg and Boris Johnson, crazy. Rightly, they didn't believe that the UK should be holding a Sword of Damocles over EU workers in Britain. It was one of the few examples of where business and the harder Brexiteers were in lockstep on an issue and, on reflection, much more could have been made of this moment from both sides to bring them together and understand each other's position.

On 26 June 2017, the Prime Minister set out the UK government's position. Theresa May announced that she wanted EU citizens living in the UK to stay after Brexit as she announced plans designed to put their 'anxiety to rest'. All EU nationals lawfully resident for at least five years would be able to apply for settled status and be able to bring over their spouses and children. Those who came after an as-yet-unagreed date would have two years to 'regularise their status', but with no guarantees. In my own business I had seen the effects of this indecision and politicking. Many of the EU citizens who had come to work at Cicero started to question their future work eligibility rights on the day after the referendum. Some employees applied for UK citizenship and many others simply left to live and work in the EU. For businesses large and small, the issue of 'settled status' for their employees was to be one which would exasperate and exacerbate the tensions of the Brexit negotiations for months.

Days after the referendum in 2016, I had walked out of my office in the heart of the City of London to get a sandwich. As I queued to pay for my lunch, I overheard a young Italian banker say to his UK colleague: 'It just doesn't feel the same any more being in London. I'm looking at moving to Dublin or perhaps back to Italy. But I'm sad about that as I would rather build my life in London.' I walked back to the office with that sadness and reflected that there were probably countless similar conversations taking place across the UK and the EU. Speaking to me for this book, Luigi Ippolito, the London correspondent of Italian newspaper *Corriere Della Sera*, said:

> That conversation was very common. Italians are the third-largest immigrant population in the UK with over 700,000 residents. Every Italian family knows a family member or friend or colleague who works or lives in the UK. That is why the level of interest in the Brexit debate and on the issue of residency is so high.

That summer, I caught my usual break in the depths of August and escaped the paralysis of the Brexit conversation. For over a decade now we have travelled to the south of France to spend time in Nice; its heady mix of summer sunshine and proximity to the artisanal agricultural and artistic joys of Provence suits us just fine. But there was to be no escaping Brexit. Like many who flew out of the UK at that time hoping to escape the mental turmoil of the UK–EU debate, we were greeted by countless questions about what we thought it might mean and where it would end. Even outside the EU, when I am in Washington or New York or Singapore, the questions remain the same. There is no relief, no escape for any of us anywhere these days. In the smartphone era, I have a technique which allows me to escape politics and business when I am on holiday. I simply switch off my internet and email roaming for most of the day, except for one hour in which I review emails and catch up with the never-ending Brexit dramas. It means for most of my day I can relax and escape the madness.

However, back in London – smartphone roaming switched back on – I headed to No. 10 to see the business relations team. As mentioned earlier, the team had lost its lead, Chris Brannigan, as part of the clear-out with Timothy, Hill and Godfrey following the election. The role would not be filled for almost a year, until City veteran dealmaker William Vereker arrived in the summer of 2018. So, I met Jimmy McLoughlin – former technology guru at the IoD – who had been with Theresa May in Downing Street from the very start. Through all the Brexit negotiations, McLoughlin has been a really effective 'pressure valve' for most businesses coming to see government to vent their frustration and propose some workable solutions. His affable, pro-business approach has kept the door open to government at times when many businesses felt like giving up. McLoughlin also masterminded many of the business delegations to Asia, the US and further afield with the Prime Minister, which at least allowed corporate and SME leaders to spend time with Theresa May and tell her what they were really feeling. I didn't mince my words when we met, telling him:

> I am seeing business now put in the time and the effort and spend the money to relocate. While the moves are small at the moment they may be ramped up if it looks like there is going to be a hard exit. The plans are like a dial on a control panel. You can turn the dial up and you can turn the dial down – it all depends on whether the politics takes us to a hard or a soft outcome. But firms are ready to do that.

He asked me about my own speciality, the City and finance. I noted the City was considerably happier with the much more serious dialogue with Steve Barclay than his predecessor, Simon Kirby. I also noted that, while politicians immediately always focus on the impact that any relocation announcement has on jobs, there would be a wider impact:

> The key driver of boardroom decisions – any decisions – is the cost of capital. Simply put – is it going to be more or less expensive to keep business in the UK as a result of Brexit? Would there be higher barriers and higher costs by staying put after Brexit? That is the main thing that business will focus on.

I suggested to McLoughlin that should be the key determinant of how business will view the government's actions. Throughout the meeting, he went into scribbling overdrive and said he would feed the thinking across government.

Before the 2017 Tory Party conference, on 22 September 2017, Theresa May delivered her next keynote Brexit address: the 'Florence speech'. Why Florence? As May's spokesman explained at the time, Florence is 'a city known for its historical trading power', the Renaissance and a 'cradle of capitalism' which drew its immense power from its banking system. But as Mark Dearn noted in *The Independent* the day before the speech, May had another subtext to the speech: 'After flourishing for a century, the [Florentine] system collapsed. Then, led by radical preacher Savonarola, Florentine society infamously rejected ostentatious high-finance wealth in the "bonfire of the vanities".[24] This would be classic, symbolic Mayism. Project the opportunities of global trade and, at the same time, have a sceptical eye cocked towards those 'masters of finance' who backed Remain! A crucial dynamic to the speech was a commitment towards a post-Brexit transition period with the EU. This had been a key lobbying issue for business: secure a deal which allows UK business the time to adjust.

Former Barclays and TheCityUK chair John McFarlane told me:

Transition was my concept. It was vital that government understood that business would need the time to be able to adjust. It was also about ensuring there would be no

---

24 Mark Dearn, 'It's no coincidence Theresa May chose Florence as the location for her Brexit speech tomorrow', *The Independent*, 21 September 2017.

shocks to the system. We had gone through all of that a decade earlier with the financial crisis and there was no appetite to do that again.

Transition was not a word the Prime Minister was going to use herself. For her it reeked of Remainerism. So her speech referred to the concept – for the first time – of an 'implementation period'. May said that it would be highly unlikely that the UK and EU would be able to have new trading arrangements in place for 29 March 2019 – the day on which the UK was supposed to leave the EU – but a period of implementation would be in the 'mutual interest' of people and businesses. She proposed that such a period, during which access to markets would continue on 'current terms', would allow business to have to plan for only one set of changes. The plan was to last for a time-limited period of around two years and have a 'double lock'.

The lobbying had worked. There had been a big push inside government to adopt the more 'cliff-edge' style Brexit, but it had been rejected by the Prime Minister. One of the striking features of the past few years and the Brexit debate was that politicians always wanted to use different words from businesspeople – but the key concept of transition had not been lost in translation. This was to be a vital part of the negotiations ahead and most business planned on being able to use the same market access arrangements, unchanged, until at least the end of 2020. The concept of transition was not only to prove to be a guiding force for May in the months ahead, but also for business when the final deal was secured in the late autumn of 2018. While the EU Withdrawal Agreement and that future Political Declaration were far from perfect in the eyes of most business leaders, the deal would secure the transition that everyone wanted to see.

Florence re-emphasised May's red lines that she had articulated in Lancaster House about the single market and the customs union which disappointed most business leaders, but she set out an ambition for a future 'economic partnership' with the EU that was to become the basis of the Political Declaration one year later. It meant a rejection of the Norway model tightly aligned to the EU and of a Canada-style deal as a restriction on 'mutual market access'.

My political risk analysis team led by Cicero director John Rowland had created the concept of the 'Brexometer' earlier in 2017. This was an analytical tool Rowland and his colleagues had been using to depict to business the chances of a hard or softer Brexit outcome. A simple gauge, the tool was reminiscent of the Bob McKenzie 'swingometer' developed decades earlier for the TV election broadcasts to show the swing between the two big parties and their chances of entering Downing Street. Rowland's Brexometer moved distinctly towards the left of the dial that day – it showed that transition and a softer Brexit had grained traction with policymakers in the UK and in the EU, and business would have more time to plan ahead. Alongside this, the government believed that the EU would want to lean towards a new security partnership with the UK, given the UK's leadership on the issue and the historical geopolitical stance it had taken as the most Atlanticist of European states. More than that, the UK government was actually lobbying itself, as it wanted the UK defence sector to play a vital part in the negotiations by showcasing Britain's capabilities in that arena.

Back in London, there was detailed lobbying work taking

place across Whitehall with business. As we have learned, the City had at last broken out of its attachment to the EU passport. The lobbying effort had become more realpolitik. TheCityUK and the Corporation of London had created the International Regulatory Strategy Group some years before Brexit to make the case for ongoing regulatory reform. Through Brexit, the group, above all others in the City, had come into its own. It was now chaired by the former Tory City minister Mark Hoban. I had noted that since he'd left politics to pursue a City non-executive career, Hoban had a healthy equidistance between the City's demands and understanding the politics. He would be a good navigator of the arguments. Speaking to me for this book, Hoban said: 'Because of their familiarity with Brussels and its ways and their own political preferences, too many people in the City remained emotionally committed to the passport for too long.'

He reflected on the Barney Reynolds plan for the City around 'enhanced equivalence': 'Barney did a great job in highlighting the issues and getting the City to move on from the idea of the passport, but Barney's plan was flawed. It didn't work for everyone – it didn't work for every business. We needed to bring everyone together and create a strong lobby.'

Hoban had set to work with City law firm Hogan Lovells to create an analysis of the EU's existing third-country structures.[25] 'We needed to give the EU a critique of equivalence – especially that it is not a stable concept for the UK,' he told me. What he meant was that equivalence arrangements could be unpicked by political decision makers in the EU at will.

---

25 Mark Hoban and Rachel Kent, 'The EU's Third Country Regimes and Alternatives to Passporting', The International Regulatory Strategy Group.

Working together with Rachel Kent, a leading partner at Hogan Lovells, they created a new plan. They called it 'mutual recognition' – a system that would allow continual ease of trade between the UK and the EU, based on agreed standards and dispute resolution models. Under the proposal, access would be restricted only in the event of both parties choosing to substantially diverge in standards and regulations. Unlike previous equivalence models, the mutual recognition concept which was proposed would restrict the ability of the EU to unilaterally withdraw access to its markets.

Of this plan, Kent said:

> Of course political words and legal words are not the same. Legal words need to be exact and political words can change around all the time. I had wanted to call mutual recognition 'mutual market access', but the politics and the lobbying took us towards arguing for a maximalist position to secure the most ambitious deal possible.

Hoban, who had been circulating the ideas in a manic journey of meetings in EU capitals alongside his meetings with the government, agreed: 'We were told by the Germans to go for a bold and ambitious ask (which was mutual recognition) in the first stages of the negotiation. And that is what we did.'

In the corridors of Whitehall this 'ambitious ask' was being met very positively and ideas were being fed to ministers, who rapidly agreed them. It was the perfect negotiating mandate for the UK from the direction set by the Prime Minister in Florence. Industry was starting to believe that it was being listened to for the first time for a long time. At the Tory Party conference in October 2017, Cicero had organised its usual big keynote event. A dinner with UK business leaders to meet some of the political and media actors performing in the annual drama that is the party conference season is always very enjoyable and allows everyone that chance to eat, drink and get to know each other better. This year I had invited BBC political editor Laura Kuenssberg and new City minister Steve Barclay. It was the first time that Kuenssberg was to watch the future Cabinet minister in action. Barclay made a powerful speech and gave the room the sense that government was listening. Kuenssberg asked him some tough questions about Brexit and his own future ambitions. He rose to the challenge and she later told me: 'He is one to watch. He did not put a foot wrong.' The firms who had attended the dinner also felt a lot more at ease. Despite the anger that erupted on the conference fringe from Tory Party members about the result of the 2017 election and the Conservatives' lost majority, there was a sense that the ship of state at last knew where it was going. Businesses had some kind of lifeboat to climb into in terms of government policy.

Earlier that week, at the conference, I had launched a personal initiative: *The New Blue Book*. Inspired by the mid-2000s Cameroon set, such as figures like Ed Vaizey and Michael Gove, who had edited *A Blue Tomorrow*, and by Paul Marshall and David Laws's Liberal *Orange Book*, I had wanted to collect a series of essays from leading conservative thinkers on everything from welfare reform to the built environment to a new form of share ownership. As someone with a centre-right philosophy, it appeared to me that there was nothing happening at the centre of government to fire up new ideas. Brexit was overwhelming the debate.

With a fellow Conservative colleague at Cicero, Ben Roback, I launched the book online at the Tory conference and I spoke at a packed-out meeting of the recently relaunched Tory Reform Group. Nicky Morgan, the new Treasury Select Committee chair, was also on the platform with me. The anger in the room about the failed election was palpable. Many in the room had turned up ready to debate former 'Remainers' like us. I spoke about the book and the questions were endless and invigorating. One member of the audience came up to me afterwards and said: 'I'm supposed to disagree with you and I don't. We need to get on with delivering fresh politics and policies.' I sent the book to No. 10 and heard nothing more…

Back in London, I was already using what I called my 'Jeremy Corbyn slide' with boardrooms. My team at Cicero had superimposed a picture of Corbyn waving from the steps of Downing Street as Prime Minister. I had first used the slide in the late summer of 2017 after the general election. When I used it, I got the reaction I had expected; most of the people around the table smiled. But, by November 2017, most of the smiles had disappeared. The Labour conference that autumn had set out ambitious plans for renationalising parts of the economy. They included plans to take energy and rail firms back into public ownership. There was also a hint that Labour's plans might not stop there and that other parts of the corporate sector would be under scrutiny.

With the Brexit drama continuing, business was not just preparing for Brexit but starting to turn its mind to what a Corbyn-led Labour government might look like.

11

MANSION HOUSE – THE PLAN

By the end of 2017, business was deep in its Brexit 'rewiring'. Detailed plans had been submitted to regulators and investors for their approval. Senior management was starting to think about who might need to relocate into the EU area. Meticulous and hugely expensive preparation was in full swing for many firms. By the spring of 2019, EY had estimated that the overall cost of Brexit planning to the UK's financial services sector was close to £4 billion. As ever, it was the banking sector whose plans were most advanced, but I also saw signs that the pharmaceutical and tech sectors were also well ahead of the game. Others were not – by and large, SME businesses' futures remained entirely in the hands of the politician's ability to agree and strike a deal with the EU.

Whether you had voted Leave or Remain, there was a simple economic imperative to get your business in the right shape for whatever was ahead. Indeed, stories started to emerge in the early spring of 2018 that Jacob Rees-Mogg had set up a Dublin-based subsidiary for his asset management operation Somerset Capital. At the time he said he was simply responding to client demand. Oh, the irony – and how Remainer Twitter fired itself up. But Rees-Mogg was a shrewd businessman as well as a politician. He knew what I and many other business owners knew: preparation was key. If nothing else, the regulators were telling you to do so. Dublin was a perfectly sensible choice for an asset management business that needed to configure itself to access the EU passport.

For six months, from the final quarter of 2017 to the end of March 2018, there was a growing momentum behind the idea that business and politics were both rewiring together. While business did not like the costs and the upheaval of this rupture from the status quo, it was adapting – and quickly. Our government seemed to be adjusting too. The 'red lines' were starting to become a little less red and pragmatism was beginning to prevail. The most obvious example of that was the December 2017 EU summit, which – against the odds – sealed a deal on the outline of the 'divorce' settlement which amazed most business leaders and commentators. For the first time under the May administration, business and politics seemed to be moving at a similar pace.

On 8 December 2017, little over six months after her election disaster, Theresa May struck a deal with the EU27 on the divorce bill, the rights of UK and EU citizens living across both territories and, most controversially, on a Northern Ireland 'backstop' that was to prove all her critics wrong – for a few months at least. The consensus view among business leaders was that when being led by David Davis the negotiations were going nowhere and the UK was heading towards isolation around the EU table with the clock ticking fast. However, when No. 10 got involved towards the end of

October, with the Prime Minister and her Brexit adviser Olly Robbins, things started to move.

Just a few weeks earlier, on 6 November, I had headed to the CBI annual conference, where the mood was awful among top business leaders. This annual big-business jamboree is a one-day affair that looks and feels like a party political conference. Many FTSE grandees turn up alongside the key political lobby journalists. In my job, I tend to seek out both. The lobby media turns up because the CBI always gives a big keynote opportunity to both the Prime Minister and opposition leaders of the day. Within minutes of arriving at the huge InterContinental Hotel beside the O2 Arena in London's Docklands, I was grabbed by the then Sky News political editor, Faisal Islam. We agreed to talk after the May and Corbyn speeches.

Relations between the CBI and the government had been in the doldrums for a long time. From the moment David Cameron's speech to the 2015 event had been rudely interrupted by Leave campaigners, things had gone from bad to worse. The CBI was not happy with the roll-out of the Remain campaign – its strategy or its tactics – and made its displeasure known to the Cameron team. But, as we have already observed, when Theresa May entered Downing Street it felt like the relationship with the new government entered a new phase – in the deep freeze.

The 2017 conference had begun with headlines from CBI director general Carolyn Fairbairn calling for the Prime Minister to go for a customs union-style deal with the EU. The problem was that Theresa May had explicitly ruled out that kind of arrangement ten months earlier in her Lancaster

House speech. As far as Britain's biggest business lobbying organisation was concerned, government wasn't listening. Worse than that, its views weren't being reflected in ministerial announcements. The CBI was having to resort to megaphone lobbying to make its point – that's never a great place to be for any lobbying organisation.

The 'freezing out' was in evidence a year earlier. At the 2016 Tory Party conference I attended a dinner hosted by the Institute of Directors. I was sat next to the engaging and pragmatic Allie Renison, the IoD's Brexit preparation lead. While the IoD had made clear its members desire to Remain during the referendum, it had not become a mouthpiece for the Remain campaign. It had maintained an equidistance from both sides. The IoD was nimbler and politically savvier than the CBI at that juncture under Simon Walker's leadership, and Renison had charted the best course for companies to take the pragmatic, practical steps to recognise the result of the referendum – and rewire accordingly. It was not campaigning for a rerun of the referendum debate. There was also Shanker Singham, who was to become – rather famously – the Brexiteers' favourite 'trade policy' guru working with think tanks and the government. Singham and I had a discussion over dinner about how to work out the 'services conundrum' on Brexit – i.e. that no one seemed to have cracked what to do about the UK's biggest economic slice. We resolved we would need to keep talking in the months ahead.

Also around the table was the then government chief whip, Gavin Williamson. A central figure in the drama ahead, I thought it was highly significant that he would choose to be at the IoD event as opposed to any other in a packed conference diary. He had backed Remain but was now marshalling the Tory Party's Westminster forces and was there to listen to an impressive gallery of Tory MPs – both Leavers and Remainers – in the room, as well as the business folks like me. But I noted he said very little over dinner. The job of the chief whip should be to watch and listen. That's probably why so many Tory MPs turned up! Inevitably – as is the way of modern life – he seemed engrossed in his mobile phone for much of the time. Through the speeches he remained equally impassive until someone mentioned his pet tarantula, Cronus. He smiled – rather menacingly, I thought!

Fast-forward to November 2017 again and you could feel the tension in the air when Carolyn Fairbairn introduced Theresa May onto the vast CBI stage. Having been set up to fail the CBI test on a customs union deal, the Prime Minister obliged by repeating her plan to aim for a bespoke UK deal. The room felt very uneasy and May was given a lacklustre ten-second burst of muted applause. But the CBI had even more to feel queasy about when some of the questions from the floor challenged the consensus in the room with their calls for a WTO-style Brexit. There were some boos but the CBI had discovered the reality that lots of businesses were in different places and had different needs and views. Representing a single voice was so hard to do in this period.

Laura Kuenssberg had been loudly booed when she got up to ask the Prime Minister a question in the conference hall. Britain's leading business leaders all assembled in the room had just shouted down the BBC political editor. I reflected at the time that it wasn't just politicians and business leaders whose relations were deteriorating – the same was true of the relations between business and media. (At the 2018 conference Laura's question to the Prime Minister was booed even more loudly!)

After coffee it was time for the Labour leader to speak. Having hosted major events with business and political leaders for years, I know at every major conference the organisers have to leave sufficient 'space' between the two big beasts of UK politics – the PM and the opposition leader – so they won't even meet each other and their entourages – it's both ego and optics. Each also wants to have their own media 'space' to spin to the likes of Kuenssberg and Islam their news lines for the day. This was the first time that Corbyn had addressed the CBI since he became Labour leader. I sat in the hall next to a couple of entrepreneurs who had travelled from Manchester and Leeds. They were not natural Labour supporters, but I could tell they were rather intrigued to hear from Corbyn. Maybe it was the novelty value of an avowed Marxist coming to talk to corporate Britain; maybe it was his message. Without missing a beat, he said to the businesses assembled that Labour would champion membership of the customs union and single market. Despite this not being on offer from the EU at that stage, he delighted the CBI leadership. How strange the moment was as Corbyn – with a glint in his eye – received a burst of applause almost four times longer than the Prime Minister had been given an hour earlier. How strange that the CBI appeared to be more in agreement with Labour than the Tories at that moment on Brexit. Trouble was continuing to build up.

Corbyn had seized his chance while the Cabinet was at war

and were nakedly briefing against each other in the run-up to the December EU summit. It seemed the political chances of a deal were remote. The issues which had Tory backbenchers and the ERG fizzing more than others were the prospect of the Prime Minister not granting rights to existing EU citizens to remain in the UK – something that united Rees-Mogg and Boris in their opposition – and paying the EU divorce bill. There was very little mention of the Northern Ireland border issue at that time. When it came to the summit itself, No. 10 briefed out the Sunday before the meeting that a deal was set to be done on citizens' rights, the exit bill and to create a 'backstop' on the Northern Ireland border issue if no other solution was agreed. They also suggested that this deal would provide the basis for a transition to the new arrangement lasting until December 2020.

Businesses rejoiced. The DUP did not. Within hours, DUP leader Arlene Foster – who had signed the confidence and supply pact with May and Gavin Williamson six months earlier – could see that the backstop could create different regulatory and legal settlements between mainland Great Britain and Northern Ireland. 'We don't want to see a red line down the Irish Sea,' she quickly told the media. Businesses and other political watchers spent the rest of that week analysing the relations between May and Foster. At one point during the negotiations in Brussels, May had to step out of the room with Juncker to take a call from Foster which forced the PM to go back to London and then come back to Brussels again at the end of the week to agree the final wording.

Writing this book in the spring and early summer of 2019 – with all the political water that has flowed under the bridge since then – it is still amazing to me that the DUP ever signed up to a legally binding backstop. It also remains a mystery as to why May's Cabinet – especially David Davis and Boris Johnson (who were to walk out eight months later after the Chequers Cabinet summit) ever felt able to sign up. Both of their spinners have told the media since that they were not shown the full content of the deal in order to understand it. It seems it was all rather like the 2017 Tory election manifesto that was never shown to the Cabinet until hours before it was launched. If that was indeed the case, there are two questions which are fair to ask those who sat around the Cabinet table at the time. Firstly, why didn't they ask to see the full wording before they gave their approval? Certainly, in business, any company director shares a liability for the decisions that are made. Not reading the minutes is no excuse, and nor is ignorance of the facts in that situation. Countless business leaders have been challenged on exactly that point when they have appeared in front of MPs on select committees. But – to be fair to them – the second question is: if the deal was not shared with the wider Cabinet, surely this showed how Cabinet decision making and effective collective responsibility had broken down? If that was the case and there was no trust between the Cabinet and the Prime Minister then the honourable thing to do would have been to resign there and then and speak out.

However, somehow May kept the show on the road. She had a divorce deal with the EU, a Cabinet that said at the time that they supported it and the DUP were still supplying 'confidence' to her administration. Heading into Christmas 2017, I observed a 'May bounce' among business leaders.

Perhaps her sphinx-like qualities would make this tortuous journey for Britain's firms rather smoother than had been anticipated. A Prime Minister who had started 2017 with a hardcore speech at Lancaster House about her 'red lines' was now delivering both Brexit and a transition. What was there not to like?

As 2018 opened the lobbying on the future relationship and transition had become intense. My friends started to refer to me as 'the Brexit man' – as there was little space for much else in my life. The detailed work from bodies like the International Regulatory Strategy Group to create a mutual recognition agreement was starting to pay off. That back-up plan on equivalence from Barney Reynolds remained in place and was being continually refined by its supporters inside and outside government. Other business sectors were doing the hard work too, but my sense was that the City and finance were – perhaps as always – way ahead of the game. David Davis may have been right when he told Barclays chair John McFarlane back in the autumn of 2016 that he was not worried about finance's future under Brexit. 'Finance will be fine.' McFarlane – quick as always – snapped back: 'Yes, but we may be fine from New York.'

By early 2018, that need to be in New York looked like it was a sharply receding prospect in most business plans. At the same time, government seemed to be fleshing out the agencies that would be able to deliver Brexit. The Department for Exiting the European Union – which had spent most of 2016 and early 2017 'begging, borrowing and stealing' staff from around Whitehall – had started to pick up speed and scale. In its early days it had raided the Cabinet Office, the

Treasury and the Department for Business for some of its brightest and best. Many of them had not wanted to leave their original departments. In the early days of businesses meeting DExEU, they came away with a queasiness born out of a lack of senior policymakers who appeared to have a grip on the events they were supposed to be managing. There was lots of high politics from DExEU ministers, but little substance at the time. Back in autumn of 2016, I had been at the wedding of my Cicero colleague and former Sky News executive producer Kate McAndrew and her partner, former Sky News and latterly Bloomberg business editor Dafydd Rees. It was a joyous affair in north London. Amid the dancing and celebrations, I bumped into a former school contemporary who now occupied a senior Cabinet Office role. He told me: 'The biggest problem we have is getting senior civil servants who want to join DExEU and actually do any of this Brexit stuff. Please send anyone my way that you think might want to do the job from the private sector.' The sense that 'Sir Humphrey' was a brake on government ambitions was already alive and kicking.

At the start of 2018 I had a quick winter break to recharge the batteries for the battles ahead. While I was away, Theresa May reshuffled her Cabinet following the loss of her deputy and confidant Damian Green as a result of allegations over the use of pornography on a work computer. He denied the allegations but left government after giving 'misleading statements' about the events. The resulting reshuffle was a disaster for the Prime Minister's authority, as some senior ministers like Education Secretary Justine Greening refused to be moved, leading to her resignation from government that night. Others, such as Health Secretary Jeremy Hunt, sat in Downing Street for almost two hours refusing to move departments, and the PM eventually backed down. On the same day the City lost its minister as Steve Barclay was promoted to Health minister after just seven months in the role. I – and most other City leaders – was bitterly sorry to see Steve go. He knew and cared about the future of the sector. New minister John Glen was going to have to find his feet, and quickly.

At the end of January, I briefed one of the major TheCityUK roundtable meetings on the machinations of the government, while pollster Deborah Mattinson talked about the current voter reactions. Mattinson and I had done countless briefings to the corporate sector throughout the Brexit saga. While we never knew exactly what each other would say before we entered the room, we always managed to agree on the key fundamentals. My script that day was that Theresa May had lost yet more authority and purchase on decisions while Mattinson made clear that voters on both sides of the Brexit argument were digging their trenches deeper. UK public opinion wasn't changing in any significant way.

At that meeting, several of the main UK bank chairs spoke. One of them remained totally unconvinced that the EU would be willing to go for a special deal on mutual recognition. But, unlike the Cabinet, everyone around the table remained resolved to continue to make the case for that deal. But the UK government was working hand in hand with business and had developed the bandwidth to cope with the overwhelming lobby it faced from industry inside DExEU. However, the cost of this to the ordinary day-to-day operation of government was to become obvious by the end of 2018.

Around that time I was also told about a meeting in Downing Street with business leaders with the Prime Minister and the Chancellor which had taken place right at the start of the year, before the looming reshuffle. The government knew that firms were relocating parts of their empires into the EU passporting zone in order to protect future business and to satisfy the regulators in those EU states. The Prime Minister had asked the businesses around the table to 'slow down' their relocation plans. One of the attendees in the meeting later told me:

> All of us were happy to give her that commitment at the time. We were pleased to see a deal done at the December summit and the government was listening to our ideas and working away on them as part of the wider negotiation about the future relationship. But when we saw the PM lose even more grip at the time of her Cabinet reshuffle – we simply intensified the planning and the relocations once again.

By early 2018, the group that was to become the People's Vote had begun fundraising in earnest. The bankrolling of another referendum campaign was a serious business and it was being orchestrated by many of the same faces who had been part of the Stronger In efforts in 2016. Burnt by the experience of the 2014 Scotland campaign and the 2016 Brexit referendum, I could not see many major businesses wanting to get involved. Private individuals were giving support but little of the corporate money which had been pumped into Stronger In was coming back to the table. Most firms had already spent a fortune on their Brexit plans and simply wanted to move on. As part of our rather politically ecumenical work, I invited MPs supporting a block on a no-deal Brexit in Parliament to come and talk to businesses at Cicero to give them an opportunity to hear the arguments. In the end, it was private individuals who turned up, many of them at pains to stress that they were there without the corporate backing of the organisations they worked for. The politicians were heard with respect and there was considerable head-nodding, but they left without securing any big financial commitments.

Much of the reason was that the lobbying of the UK government was now paying off and would be articulated in the forthcoming Mansion House speech of 2 March 2018. This was to be the most comprehensive depiction yet of the government's ambitions for a future trading relationship with the EU. The intensity of interest in the speech from UK and global inbound businesses created another moment of high drama for me and the Cicero team. However, the briefing in advance we had received from government was making me and the businesses we worked with feel more and more confident that the government had a strong hand to play in the discussions ahead with the EU and that they had indeed listened to business.

The early spring of 2018 was one of the coldest on record. Cabinet ministers gathered in Chequers on 22 February for the first time that year to finalise plans for the government's approach towards the next phase of the negotiations. While the weather outside was hostile, rare Cabinet unity emerged on a way forward. The briefing and counter-briefing in advance and during the meeting had become so usual that most business leaders had tuned out. However, in time for the late evening news a Cabinet deal was in sight. Remarkably, in retrospect, it again built the 'hated' backstop into the package. Was anyone in Cabinet really talking to the DUP or the ERG at that stage to gauge their appetite for the package?

Just over a week later on 2 March, the so-called Beast from the East had grounded the Prime Minister in London rather than her planned location for the grand unveiling of the strategy – Newcastle. Politicians these days always prefer a 'hard hat' moment with the TV backdrop of a factory or new tech enterprise well outside London if possible, in order to show they have escaped the bubble and are 'in touch'. The City of London, with his history and associations with the banking sector, didn't usually fit the bill. But, as the weather wasn't playing ball, the No. 10 machine reached out to find a building with gravitas. The City of London Corporation was happy to oblige with Mansion House. It's the home of the Lord Mayor of London and hosts the annual bankers banquet each June where the Chancellor of the Exchequer and Governor of the Bank of England deliver keynote speeches on the future economic trajectory, which is usually televised. Both Gordon Brown and George Osborne often spoke in a lounge suit rather than the usual black tie, as they wanted to show some distance from those bankers on the TV screens and contrast the sumptuous surroundings of Mansion House. In June 2019, I was there to witness the infamous storming of the Chancellor Philip Hammond's speech by Greenpeace, who were protesting about the climate emergency. The Mansion House has often found itself at the centre of our national life.

So, this was an important signal from Theresa May and her government that they were 'leaning in' towards the City after two years of leaning away – on public platforms, at least. It was a recognition, perhaps, of the importance of the financial services sector to the UK economy and a backdrop that would allow the Prime Minister to make a Brexit deal for services – the centrepiece of the thinking. Against a No. 10-installed backdrop, 'Our Future Partnership', May delivered a late-morning speech that truly stunned everyone listening to it, from the City grandees in the room to the politicians tuning in. It was comprehensive, balanced and – at long last – reached out to business, and it provided a framework for the negotiations ahead. Her fundamental principle was that trade with the EU should be as 'frictionless as possible'. The key principle of 'mutual recognition' was embedded in the detailed ideas for the services sector. May said:

The Chancellor will be setting out next week how financial services can and should be part of a deep and comprehensive partnership. We are not looking for passporting because we understand this is intrinsic to the single market of which we would no longer be a member. It would also require us to be subject to a single rule book, over which we would have no say.

The UK has responsibility for the financial stability of the world's most significant financial centre, and our taxpayers bear the risk, so it would be unrealistic for us to implement new EU legislation automatically and in its entirety.

But with UK located banks underwriting around half

of the debt and equity issued by EU companies and providing more than £1.1 trillion of cross-border lending to the rest of the EU in 2015 alone, this is a clear example of where only looking at precedent would hurt both the UK and EU economies.

As in other areas of the future economic partnership, our goal should be to establish the ability to access each other's markets, based on the UK and EU maintaining the same regulatory outcomes over time, with a mechanism for determining proportionate consequences where they are not maintained. But given the highly regulated nature of financial services, and our shared desire to manage financial stability risks, we would need a collaborative, objective framework that is reciprocal, mutually agreed, and permanent and therefore reliable for businesses.

At Cicero, our UK political risk director John Rowland quickly wrapped the thinking into three 'buckets', placed different industries into each and sent out a client briefing. (The buckets were also mocked up onto a slide which caused much amusement in the weeks to come as the deal turned sour. They were later referred to internally as the sick buckets.) The first bucket contained the idea of 'tight alignment' with the EU – the most likely approach for the aviation and pharmaceutical sectors. There would be no tariffs or any major differences in regulatory style and the UK would maintain associate membership of EU regulatory agencies. The second – all-important for the financial services sector – was that idea of mutual recognition which had been so ardently lobbied for in the preceding months, through which the UK would aim for the same goals as EU regulation and policy but do so through different means. In practice, this would mean a similar regulatory outcome over time and a collaborative reciprocal framework with an independent arbitration regime. The final bucket would be a regime for the digital economy where there would be significant divergence from the EU. It would allow the UK to continue to adopt an approach to regulation and tax very different to the EU one. If it looks complicated, that's because it was. But it was a speech in which the Prime Minister showed she had listened to the lobbying over the months and appeared to be the framework for the start of the next phase of the negotiations. Leaving the EU was going to be complicated – that's what business had argued – so a complex approach was perfectly reasonable. In fact, it was desirable. Westminster and business appeared to be suddenly on the same page for the first time in years.

It is worth taking some time here to mention the applause Theresa May achieved across the Brexit trenches for that speech – for those trenches would only dig themselves in deeper in the year ahead. Everyone from Jacob Rees-Mogg to the IoD purred their approval (although the CBI was once again notable with a slightly less than enthusiastic reply).

Rees-Mogg said:

This was a good speech by the Prime Minister … Mrs May is taking a sensible, pragmatic and generous approach; offering something to the EU whilst also being extremely clear on Northern Ireland, so I am content. There are inevitably a few small points that will concern Leave campaigners but we must all recognise that everyone will have to give up something to get a deal, so now is not the time to nit-pick.[26]

Given the subsequent events that unfolded on the Northern Ireland backstop, it is worth re-reading these words from the then chair of the ERG again and again! DUP leader Arlene Foster agreed, saying:

> The Prime Minister has set forward the basis upon which it would be possible to move forward. I welcome the Prime Minister's clear commitment that she will not countenance any new border being created in the Irish Sea between Northern Ireland and the rest of the United Kingdom. Securing a sensible outcome for everyone will require the EU27 to consider innovative solutions rather than rule out any proposal which has not been conceived in Brussels.[27]

So May had united the ERG and the DUP in warmly welcoming her speech. It was remarkable.

The business organisations also gave the speech a positive nod. Responding for the IoD, director general Stephen Martin commented:

> It is important that she explicitly referenced the need for binding commitments in areas such as state aid and competition policy, which the IoD has long called for.

26 Jacob Rees-Mogg, 'Leavers will have concerns with Mrs May, but now is not the time to nitpick', *Daily Telegraph*, 2 March 2018.
27 Reuters, 'Reaction to May's speech on Brexit', 2 March 2018.

Her acknowledgment of the need for new labour mobility arrangements will also strike a positive chord with businesses. On regulation, we are glad to see her refer to the importance of new cooperation mechanisms that will underpin the trust in each other's regulatory frameworks. It is important to stress that if the UK is doubling down on its unprecedented customs partnership model, HMRC (tax authorities) have said it will take five years minimum to implement. That means businesses will need longer to adjust to new settings.[28]

Even the EU seemed to be extremely positive. Lead EU negotiation commissioner Michel Barnier tweeted: 'I welcome PM @theresa_may speech. Clarity about #UK leaving Single Market and Customs Union & recognition of trade-offs will inform #EUCO guidelines re: future (free trade agreement).'

Boris Johnson, then still Foreign Secretary, tweeted: 'We will remain extremely close to our EU friends and partners – but able to innovate, to set our own agenda, to make our own laws and to do ambitious free trade deals around the world.'

Heidi Allen MP, who was less than one year later to leave the Conservatives to launch ChangeUK, eulogised: 'I'm greatly encouraged by PM's speech – categorically said WTO not acceptable, no hard border in Ireland, citizens to continue to work and study across UK/EU, science participation, mutual regs for e.g. medicine, data sharing and tariff free customs arrangement.' Remarkably, as she left the Conservatives to firmly oppose Brexit, she used the hashtag #RoadtoBrexit!

---

28 Reuters, 'Reaction to May's speech on Brexit', 2 March 2018.

Once again, the CBI maintained the most business-sceptic stance and was rather less encouraged, noting:

> The Prime Minister reiterated that the UK will remain outside a customs union with the EU, and restated the Government's previously published two potential options on customs. There was no more detail available on how either option would function but the Prime Minister described first a 'new customs partnership.' This proposal would involve firms undertaking a huge burden to enforce different tariffs on those goods that end up in the EU as opposed to the UK.[29]

It later took more flak for being so negative. However, despite the CBI, many business leaders felt as if there had been a breakthrough.

One week later I was sitting advising the annual TheCityUK board away day outside London. Chair John McFarlane and IRSG lead Mark Hoban were over the moon, alongside those assembled around the table. The campaign to argue for mutual recognition appeared to have worked. It was the UK government's starting point for the substantive negotiations on the future relationship. On the same day, in the middle of the meeting, Chancellor Philip Hammond was set to give a major speech at HSBC which would flesh out the government's thinking on financial services. The board of the top City folks listened in with some care. Notably, Hammond hedged when he referred to both equivalence and mutual

---

29 'The Business View of the Prime Minister's Mansion House Speech', CBI.

recognition. He knew the words would have differing inter-pretations in the EU and the UK. Constructive ambiguity was in play, you might say. He made the case for the UK having the ability to deliver equivalence in regulatory outcomes achieved by those different means. Underpinning this would be a system of mutual recognition and reciprocal regulato-ry equivalence, supported by dispute resolution structures. He noted that there should be clear regulatory oversight for managing future divergence to ensure reasonable and pro-portionate regulatory responses. I sensed the room shudder somewhat. Those easily interchangeable terms for the politi-cians – 'mutual recognition' and 'equivalence' – were words with specific consequences for businesses and had caused so much rancour over the previous year inside the industry. Nevertheless, the sense was that the Treasury and No. 10 were in alignment about the future negotiations ahead and that the UK was about to 'go into bat' with Brussels on the basis of the Mansion House speech. It appeared to be a great outcome.

As the weather – politically and meteorologically – im-proved around Easter 2018, I sat down for breakfast with No. 10 business liaison special adviser Jimmy McLoughlin. He was about to get married in the summer of 2018 and – like the rest of us – was suffering from the ongoing dramas of the Brexit negotiations. I was pleased for him that a big per-sonal celebration ahead would restore and renew. We met in Westminster and I enjoyed another Indian-themed breakfast at the Cinnamon Club. (It is an often-repeated complaint that there are very few places to go for a meal around the precincts of Whitehall and Westminster. I have long thought that needs to be remedied.) He told me:

Everyone keeps predicting that the next summit is going to be a failure. That the next big speech is going to disappoint. We are now locked in a series of ten- to twelve-week negotiating cycles where most of the time business and the commentators are filled with gloom and doom and the sense is that there is another looming crisis just around the corner. Then – each time – the Prime Minister pulls it out of the bag.

In the early spring of 2018, it felt just like that. Better weather and a summer of private and royal weddings were just around the corner. But somewhere at the back of our minds there was just that niggling question of the Northern Ireland backstop…

12

WHAT HAPPENED TO THE PLAN?

Almost as soon as the Mansion House speech was delivered, UK policymakers seemed to stop talking about it. The Cabinet rapidly turned in on itself on the issue of the Irish border and a heated debate about so-called magical solutions took place. The EU Commission, in the guise of Michel Barnier who had so positively welcomed the Prime Minister's approach on the day of her speech, rapidly started to trash the workability of the plan and politicians everywhere started to fall out.

It reminded me of that 'historic' moment in February 2016 when David Cameron had secured his deal with the EU. It was a huge media event but days later the headlines from the deal had become consigned to 'fish and chip wrapping', as the older hacks used to say. Perhaps political 'Snapchat' would be a better term in this digital age – ideas which appear to be so alive one moment and then just fizzle out. Mansion House had been presented in similar ways to business as 'historic' and a kind of 'peace in our time' with the EU, but it rapidly proved to be no more than another short chapter in the never-ending crisis.

However, if the politicians in the UK and the EU didn't

want to talk about it, business certainly did. Mansion House was the high-water mark of the lobbying over the two years since the Brexit vote. After the emotion following the 2016 result, it had brought together disparate industries, relieved much of the pressure on the intense rewiring and planning and, just one year from the planned exit date, provided politicians on all sides with something to get behind. Yet within weeks – perhaps even within days – my conversations in Whitehall with officials on behalf of business made me increasingly nervous yet again. Our Cicero notes to clients in April 2018 – less than six weeks after the speech – said:

> There is no heavy lifting going on around the deal between the UK and the EU right now. Rather than pushing hard, it looks like British officials have just given up the fight while they await the UK Cabinet to sort out the situation for goods on the Irish border. As far as I can see, services are being ignored – for now.

My hope was that after the intense debate about the Irish border, we would soon get back to the plan. It proved to be a dream rather than a reality.

So why were officials in London so reluctant to push hard? Around that time, one top-ranking Whitehall official told me: 'The problem goes way back before Brexit. Things have been difficult for years. It was just the Brexit negotiations which exposed this. Since the veto by David Cameron in December 2011 a lot of trust was lost. The Brexit vote just opened up the wounds.' These words reflected what I had heard earlier from the finance sector, too.

The reason the UK – and all business lobbying – had shot for an ambitious new deal with the EU was because individual member states had told us to do just that. It made sense. In this case, UK business and government had spent months negotiating with each other and had come to a settled position. It had not been easy. There had been huge mistrust and anger after the referendum and the times when the new May administration had shut business out had only made things worse, but domestic relations had rapidly improved by spring 2018. The UK trade business groups and some of the largest UK businesses with EU footprints had been beating a path to the door of individual member states one by one and had been given a pretty positive welcome to their lobbying position. This seemed to show that some key member states, including Germany, did want to talk directly to the UK and to British businesses. In public, EU leaders continued to mouth words about 'solidarity' to satisfy Juncker and Tusk, but the reality was that there were conversations to be had. And they were happening. Of course, as events unfolded later in 2018, those conversations were to prove to be utterly wasted as the UK Cabinet continued to fight among itself rather than take the debate to the EU negotiating table. For a brief moment, the UK had an opportunity to gain an advantage in the negotiations. It was lost. The enmity inside the UK Cabinet has been a disaster for Britain. Our civil servants negotiating for the UK were trapped.

Miles Celic, CEO of TheCityUK, told me:

On our plan around mutual recognition, we were told by international trade experts to go for a maximalist negotiating starting point. Not to start with equivalence. In 2018 from David Davis's UBS speech, followed by the PM's Mansion House speech, it was clear that the industry position had won round the UK government. Everyone was aligned in the UK in the same place. It was remarkable.

Mark Hoban – who along with his IRSG group had brought together the City of London's highly disparate voices – told me: 'We needed at the start of the negotiations about the future relationship to make a bold and ambitious ask. The UK government was telling us to do that, and so were individual EU member states. So that's what we did.'

What – according to Celic – was more remarkable was that the UK government hardly bothered to talk about the proposed new deal for services after that point. 'It appeared we were doing all the lobbying in the EU for the UK position after 2 March,' said Celic. While statements from UK government ministers to countless business events in the UK continued to emphasise the mutual recognition approach, it quickly became clear that the UK government had caved in at the sign of the earliest resistance from EU Commission officials. The idea of a no-holds-barred full-frontal negotiation was a mirage. Britain was suddenly not even going into bat for its own agreed position!

Around the time of the Mansion House speech, I met up with one of the UK's pre-eminent financial sector magic circle lawyers, Clifford Chance's Simon Gleeson. Gleeson and I had known of each other for years, but we had never sat down to meet one-to-one. It felt like an appropriate time to do so and share. Gleeson had been working with the sector as well as advising G20 governments (including the UK) and financial regulators on financial policy. Just like Barney Reynolds, Gleeson was a deep thinker, but came at the issues from a very different perspective. In his view, Brexit was bound to make life very complicated. We both agreed that a deal with the EU, while not impossible, was going to be difficult to arrange – not least because of the politics. Gleeson also said that he, like me, had been beavering away with firms aiming to get them 'Brexit ready'. He indicated that almost one year out from 29 March 2019 firms needed to be able to satisfy their regulators in the UK and EU that the pipe would work after Brexit Day.

Gleeson was right. At that point – in the very midst of the launch of the UK's big offer to the EU – my business was deeply engaged in the detail of that rewiring, especially for the banking sector. It was also becoming clear that the UK regulators were finding it much more difficult to get assurances from their EU counterparts that UK firms would be able to continue to do business in the same way in a no-deal situation. Two vital issues were coming into sharp relief for the City. One, for the huge global asset management sector, was 'delegation'. Put simply, this meant the ability to have most of the fund managers actually managing the money based in London – as they had done while the UK remained a member of the EU – and not have to be based inside the EU area. The other was that of 'contract continuity'. Would contract laws – especially important for the insurance sector and the derivatives market and which are currently underpinned by law in the UK as a direct result of EU membership – continue to have legal force after Brexit? For these two huge industries, being able to keep staff in London and manage money globally was vital. Ensuring insurance contracts would actually have legal force was a wider threat to the very existence of the sector. But while UK ministers and UK regulators pressed their case, EU politicians and their regulators didn't move an inch for most of 2018.

I sat down with a senior board member of one of the City regulators not long after the Mansion House speech, who told me: 'The EU supervisory authorities are just unable to move. They would love to sort out contact continuity and delegation rules – but they tell us that they can't right now until the politicians work it out.' I recalled what then Financial Conduct Authority chairman John Griffith-Jones had told the City in July 2017 – that without the politics, the process would have been so much easier!

The City and other business sectors were to spend the rest of 2018 trapped in the same place. No-deal planning became the safest place to be and the money being spent on preparation intensified. As Christian May told me: 'The speed with which the City adapted to Brexit – for all that it may have lamented it – was extraordinary. It did so faster than any other sector of the economy.'

There is an old adage in business to 'follow your customer', and by the spring of 2018 the Cicero Group board had already taken that decision. We had operated in Brussels for over a decade, but we needed to ensure that our customers would have a 'home' EU member state option for the lobbying ahead. That wasn't a political choice for a businessman like me; it was just good business. The constant refrain I heard was that business did not want to become EU 'rule takers' after the UK had left the EU, so we needed to devise a way through to influencing EU decision making from the inside. Being only in Brussels was akin to operating in the US only from Washington DC. (Old lobbying hands often refer to it as 'Brussels DC'.) It is not really a place that has the authority to move the political debate. You needed to have political representation and lobbying outside the political 'beltway' and in a home member state.

As I have already mentioned, back in the summer of 2016 we had started our reconnaissance in Ireland. By late 2017 it was clear we needed to have a Brexit-proofed option, and by then it was obvious to us it was going to be Dublin rather than any other EU location. There were many reasons for that choice, but the key one was the preponderance of our clients moving operations to Dublin to be ready for Brexit. We moved quickly to find an office with Cicero CEO Jeremy Swan, EU director Helena Walsh and talent director Parisa Namazi shuttling to and from Dublin to set up the new operation.

Weeks before we launched in March 2018, Helena Walsh and I found ourselves being given the 'green carpet' treatment in the Irish capital, meeting key politicians and receiving tangible support for our launch from the superb Irish Development Agency (IDA). Sitting in the IDA CEO Martin Shanahan's office in February 2018 was the start of a maelstrom of activity ahead. Shanahan and I posed for a picture in front of the Irish and EU flags. Launching any new business venture is exciting, but this time the symbolism was heady. The support for businesses from the IDA was something to behold and it is something that other countries should take a close look at – it is impressive.

Just a month later we launched Cicero Ireland to much media fanfare, with a reception in Dublin with Irish Business Minister Pat Breen TD. Breen spoke to a room filled with UK and Irish businesses and the reticence about overtly promoting Ireland that we had seen from Irish ministers in the summer and autumn of 2016 was already a distant memory. By now the Irish inward investment marketing machine was in full swing and showing tangible signs of success. The lessons of the previous decade ('brass-plating') had been learned by the Irish authorities and UK businesses were setting up on a significant scale. It was clear that was already causing yet more headaches for a newly overheating Dublin property market. But, through Dublin, the route into the EU market and the all-important EU single market passport had been secured for many firms. UK and EU regulators were satisfied, and customers would be offered a seamless transition to Dublin in many cases. Business had by now moved way ahead of the politicians.

I am often asked by pro-Brexit politicians why business remained so wedded to the EU passport and was not willing to embrace the new opportunities. The answer remains simple. Business can only operate within the context of a known and secured legal and fiscal regime. While policymakers squabbled over the putative new basis for the UK–EU divorce and had still not even baked the new settlement on which trade might take place between the UK and the EU, business could only deal with the laws and taxes it could see. Therefore, the passport was the only basis on which firms could operate. Yes, business often finds the status quo easier, but it also needs to have a secure legal and regulatory framework under which to operate. During 2017 and 2018 it had done its best to provide the UK Cabinet with positive ideas to secure just that. The horizon to the new world of Brexit opportunity remained deeply shrouded in Cabinet mist.

Back in London I had recently become a non-executive director of the global fintech body Innovate Finance, which was set up in partnership with the City of London Corporation and the government when George Osborne had been Chancellor. Osborne had recognised the importance of the fintech sector as a mechanism to continue to keep the UK and the City as the leading place to set up and grow a financial services business. It would be the future of the financial sector. While Osborne had trumpeted the sector and the Financial Conduct Authority put in place world-leading regulation to stimulate it, fintech was not sensing a lot of love from politicians, who were maxed out on Brexit. This was to prove to be a familiar tale for so many business sectors.

Every spring, Innovate Finance hosts a global summit and organises UK Fintech Week for the UK government. Over 3,000 people attend events across the UK capital with hundreds flying in from the US west coast and Asia to seek out new fintech firms and ideas. The event takes over the grand Guildhall building in the centre of the City of London, where the sneakers of fintech meet the suits of corporate finance. The energy in the room crackles with opportunity and deals get done. In the final week of March 2018, the mood was incredibly positive. By then the UK government had got with the programme and was once again championing the opportunities ahead. I chaired a panel with the CBI director general Carolyn Fairbairn, who gave the audience perhaps the most pro-government thoughts I had heard from the CBI since the spring of 2016. In a departure from her previous script, Fairbairn positively purred about the Mansion House speech just a few short weeks earlier. I could tell from those in the room they felt that Brexit was pretty much being sorted. It was time to move on to other things.

New City minister John Glen came to address the summit. Glen was also the MP for Salisbury and had his own bandwidth issues at that time, dealing with an international diplomatic and security crisis on his patch. Despite not quite having the initial passion for the City as Barclay, Glen was a hard-working minister who mastered the brief quickly and gave the sector similar confidence. But almost as soon as he was in position, he faced that national security crisis in the heart of his own Salisbury constituency as a result of the poisoning of former Russian military officer Sergei Skripal and his daughter Yulia with the deadly nerve agent Novichok. Needless to say, Glen was distracted when he came to speak to the Guildhall sneakers and suits.

Nevertheless, despite the horror of events in his own seat, Glen used the speech to underline the government's approach towards getting an ambitious deal with the EU. Glen was still repeating that same line just hours before the infamous Chequers summit in July 2018. As we shall see, these public commitments masked the horror show of the Cabinet meltdown that was taking place over goods and the Irish border question, and was to deeply unsettle business, who thought the UK government was now negotiating in earnest on the basis of the Mansion House plan. It was the constant pattern of this stop-start activity at the heart of government that had made business most jumpy. There were no guarantees from the politicians. Trust was in short supply.

In order to change gear from Brexit and to lighten the mood for business and myself, I hosted a breakfast at Cicero at the start of the Commonwealth Heads of Government Meeting in London in late April. The 'Beast from the East' had long departed and London was enjoying a fabulously warm spring. One of my personal passions is harnessing the power of business to do good. So I invited then Home Secretary Amber Rudd to come and join me with some of the UK's biggest money managers, including Schroders CEO Peter Harrison, Legal & General's head of personal investing Helena Morrissey and human rights NGOs including the LGBT lobby group Stonewall (for which I am proud to be an ambassador) and global LGBT giving platform GiveOut (for which I am a trustee).

With some thirty of us around the table, Rudd spoke about her ambitions for the summit and we applauded the focus of the UK government on promoting LGBT human rights across Commonwealth nations. That week the government was to make this a major focus of the agenda. The legacy of British colonial law had not been a good one for LGBT people across the Commonwealth, with thirty-six countries still retaining draconian anti-LGBT laws. But after just one hour of discussion with some of the UK's biggest investors, there was agreement to support the government in making change happen in some of the countries most affected. Unlike Brexit, it felt like everyone in the room was able to breathe together and that business and politics could work together – on this at least.

Rudd's ministerial car drove her away from Cicero on the morning of 16 April 2019 directly back to the Home Office and the Windrush debate that was to sweep her from office just days later. A brief moment of unanimity had been achieved, but Rudd's imminent departure from government meant we would have to start again on this particular lobby. The ministerial merry-go-round was upon us yet again. *Plus ça change*, I thought!

In early March 2018 I bumped into former IoD media man Andy Silvester, who had just arrived at *The Sun* as one of their lead column writers, at a media party hosted by *PRWeek*. Andy was in rare form. He was thoroughly enjoying working in 'Murdochland'. I asked him what he and *The Sun* thought of the current situation. His response told me everything: 'The PM is living on borrowed time since the 2017 election – numbers wise. My suspicion is that we will back her until 29 March 2019 when Brexit is finally delivered. After that – who knows?'

13

PARTY TIME AND BREXITCASTING

While the Brexit negotiations were going nowhere, the sun was at least shining and the weather was improving by May 2018. It was also time for me to step back from Brexit and enjoy a few days off to celebrate being fifty years old! I had agonised over whether to have a party – whether to just quietly slip into my next half-century or to do so with a bit of a bang. Not least to relieve the Brexitmania, I needed a drink and my friends did too. So, I gathered together friends, colleagues, clients and others from the wider hinterland of my first half-century for a rather swell party at The Ivy in London's Covent Garden. Well, you are only fifty once! To allow readers of this book a little breather from the Brexit and business angst on these pages, let me tell you the story.

I had been going to The Ivy for exactly half my life since I arrived in London as a young journalist and struck a real bond with its impresario Fernando Peire. The restaurant is right in the centre of theatreland, and theatre is a personal passion. It is my and my other half's escapism from the workaday realities of life and I cherish it in these days of ongoing political crisis more than ever. The Ivy is a beautiful art deco gem in the centre of London and has played host to celebrities, politicians and business folk for years. It truly is a melting pot served together with fantastic food.

Well, my party certainly started with a bang – but not quite the one I had intended – as one of my guests spectacularly collapsed with a thud on the polished parquet floor, passing out right in the middle of the room. It took some time to revive her and get medical attention. After awaiting an ambulance, Fernando Peire had to walk to the nearby Shaftesbury Avenue Fire Station to get paramedic help. When two tall firemen arrived to revive my fallen guest, there was some speculation that something more outrageous had been set up for my birthday. I hasten to add the firemen kept their clothes firmly on.

A lot of my friends in my political and business life stem from my birthplace in Aberdeen and my education in Scotland. Celebrating with me that night were guests including Cameron's comms guru Craig Oliver; Craig and I had lived in Aberdeen and went to St Andrews University over the same period, before studying together in Cardiff at the university's journalism school. The new MP for Aberdeenshire West and Kincardine (the place my family had lived for all my adult life) Andrew Bowie MP also shared the celebrations. After years of being in the wilderness, the Scots Tories were back, and I was delighted to know Andrew. His energy and enthusiasm as a new MP was quickly spotted by the Tory whips' office and by the end of 2018 he had been appointed as Theresa May's PPS – her parliamentary bag carrier and eyes and ears. Of course, I was also thrilled to host then Aberdeen Standard CEO Martin Gilbert – we went to the same school in Aberdeen, Robert Gordon's College, and he had been taught by my mum's brother. Of course, we shared our school with Michael Gove – a man I have made a career out of cheekily impersonating in after-dinner speeches!

Mingling with me that night were Chief Secretary to the Treasury Liz Truss and Aberdeen Standard chair Gerry Grimstone, who had arrived with Martin. Gerry had worked as Margaret Thatcher's privatisation guru. Liz and Gerry had become firm friends over the previous year after meeting at the Tory Party conference in 2017 for the first time. I watched as they both nattered intensely at the party and wondered what new policies Liz would be cooking up. Both were passionate about trade, and Liz was to become Boris Johnson's first Trade Secretary the following year. Liz and I had known each other for over a decade since she had been the deputy director of the Reform think tank. I had helped her prepare for her selection as a Tory candidate and had also helped her and Sajid Javid launch the backbench Free Enterprise Group with a reception at the 2011 Tory conference. *Private Eye* picked up on the launch at the time, marking both out for future success.

Liz is politically fearless and is also genuinely interested in new ideas and a new way forward for Tory politics. She also was and remains highly pro-enterprise. Speaking to me for this book while Chief Secretary to the Treasury, she told me that she wanted to portray herself as a kind of 21st-century Ronald Reagan-esque figure in UK political life. Reagan had once said: 'The nine most terrifying words in the English language are "I'm from the government and I'm here to help".' Truss told me in the summer of 2019: 'We need to be more like Ronald Reagan right now.'

Also celebrating with me that night was National Portrait

Gallery (NPG) director general Nick Cullinan. I had got to know Nick only in the previous year by becoming a patron at the gallery. Since the Brexit referendum we have talked on and off and he tells me he sees the job of the NPG and other iconic British culture landmarks as critical to 'making the nation feel happy again'. In early 2019, the NPG exhibition of iconic British photographer Martin Parr, 'Only Human', was just amazing. A riot of colour and a big shout-out to all parts of Britain – Brexiteer or Remainer; upper, middle or working class – it was an attempt to celebrate all that we have. In the spring of 2019, as I was writing this book, I went back again and again to see it for its sense of hopefulness and joy.

After the big birthday celebrations, I headed off to the US for a week of rest. Being fifty had started with a bang and there was more excitement to come. After a couple of days of partying in New York I woke up in our Brooklyn hotel room with its fine view of Manhattan to find my half-century frame was in agony as my back had given way. Months and months of hyper-manic Brexit gazing had taken its toll. I writhed around in agony on the hotel floor as my partner Mark Twigg called the emergency services. Yet more firemen arrived into my life for the second time in a week! This time they were of the New York Fire Department variety. While I was busy screaming in pain, they asked me which hospital I would like to be taken to. My response was screamed clearly through the agony: to take me to the nearest emergency room. After some heated argument they advised that it would be better to drive into Manhattan – that I would be 'more comfortable' there. This was clearly a reflection of both the workings of the American health system and the belief – of two native New Yorkers – that I would be better off in an emergency room in Manhattan with more middle-class faces. It was quite an indictment of the US system.

So – after Mark had rapidly packed up our entire hotel room in just ten minutes – off we drove in the NYPD ambulance into Manhattan. I writhed in agony on every bump and grind in the road and into the Manhattan mid-town tunnel. We quickly arrived at the University Hospital emergency room and received all that I knew I might need – supercharged pain-killing drugs, co-codamol, and something to relax the mind, which appeared to be diazepam. As I lay on a hospital trolley for my short stay, my partner paid the bill. Overall, the two-and-a-half-hour stay and the drugs were to cost around $6,000. When we travelled back to the UK, I hit Twitter and thanked our clinicians for the NHS!

Despite my brief encounter with the US health system, I then hobbled to LaGuardia Airport and we flew to Florida, taking a few more days to rest by the beach. Rather than the more exciting plans we had, I spent most of the time exercising in the swimming pool in order to get my back into top form to travel back to the UK. But it had been time away from the political madness.

Around the same time amid the confusion of Brexit, which had been driving our clients crazy, things were going well for us and we had spotted an opportunity to acquire another business to increase Cicero's scale and deepen our impact lobbying across the wider economy. In April 2018, an old political and lobbying friend James Bethell approached me, Cicero CEO Jeremy Swan and our corporate advisers, SI Partners. SI had been working with Cicero for a couple of years, getting our business match-fit to continue to expand. They also knew that Bethell, the son of a hereditary Tory peer and former MEP, whose opportunity to take a seat in the House of Lords would be up for grabs in a forthcoming Lords by-election. Since the Blair government removed most of the hereditaries from the House of Lords in 1999, places have only become available in a by-election when peers in that group die or retire from the House. Bethell had tried to be elected a few years earlier without success. He later told me that owning and running his lobbying business, Westbourne Communications, had been a barrier to his election to the Lords. So when a by-election was called, and with Bethell having a very good chance of success, he had resolved to sell it to us.

For Cicero, here was an opportunity to do a fantastic deal which would catapult our business into becoming the UK's biggest independent lobbying consultancy. I was there at the start of the negotiations to talk about the opportunity, but I left the financial engineering and the brilliant deal making to Jeremy Swan, who is a master of these things, and our advisers at SI Partners, led by the exceptional Joe Hine. By the time I returned from the US the deal was almost ready to sign and we announced the tie-up to the press. Bethell and I decided to abandon the typical and rather boring men-in-suits handshake. We went down to the 'bouncy' Millennium Bridge across the Thames between St Paul's and the Tate Modern and had a hilarious time having shots taken embracing each other with a hearty hug; Bethell was later to call it the 'huggle'. The press loved it and we had certainly caught the media imagination of the moment.

The very same week, Westbourne held its annual grand

party at the Institute of Contemporary Arts on the Mall. Hundreds of guests flowed into the celebration, including then Culture Secretary Matt Hancock, Labour's Daniel Zeichner and Liz Truss – of course! There was a hilarious moment when James Bethell announced that he had been hoping that Brexit Secretary David Davis would be able to attend, but he understood that Davis would be rather busy. Almost at that very moment Davis walked into the room right behind Bethell and the party erupted with laughter.

As the wine flowed, I spoke to Davis, who was in as chipper a mood as ever. We were speaking just days in advance of the Chequers showdown set to take place in early July with the Cabinet at the Prime Minister's country retreat. He remained confident that a deal could be done with the EU, but the question on my mind was, what kind of deal? Davis had been out and about that week explaining that his approach was to attempt to create some kind of 'mini union' with the EU which might provide access to the EU market. Of course, the Prime Minister had another deal in mind – one that was more akin to a customs union, for goods at least.

Towards the end of the party, I bumped into No. 10 Europe special adviser Denzil Davidson, who had come along for a well-earned drink. He was deep in the preparation for the Chequers meeting and – rightly – really didn't want to be drawn into detail. But in response to me asking him what the ambition for the talks was, he said: 'We are aiming to have the "best" third country relationship with the EU of any third country.' Davidson was either pointing towards Davis's Canada+++ idea, which would mean a hard Brexit and an arm's-length relationship with the EU based on reducing tariffs and trade barriers and harmonising regulations, or pointing towards the customs union. He used language which was as inscrutable as that of his boss. Both sides in the Cabinet meeting ahead would only know where she was heading when they actually got to Chequers.

The following week, Laura Kuenssberg called me up and asked if I would appear on the brilliant BBC 5 Live Brexitcast podcast. It was on the day that the Queen was just about to sign her royal assent after the tortuous journey of the EU Withdrawal Bill. Brexit was becoming real. Signed into law was legislation which would transpose EU law into UK law as our starting point but that would begin the journey of allowing the UK to start its divergence from the EU after Brexit. Both sides in the Tory Party were able to claim victory and to say that the government had a 'stable' plan. It also appeared at that time that the so-called Norway option – membership of the European Economic Area – had been killed off.

I headed down to the BBC's Westminster studios in Millbank and met Laura. After we got a single-use plastic cup of BBC tea, she guided me into the small radio studio where Brexitcast is recorded. I have to admit I was really excited. The podcast was becoming a huge hit with listeners and was one of the top ten downloads on the new BBC Sounds app. The presenters also knew that Westminster and the EU Commission were listening to the show by now.

I think I was the first 'lobbyist' to appear on the show and this was an opportunity to talk about what business wanted to see from the negotiations ahead. What I had noted was that the government had shifted to a 'five minutes to midnight' plan with MPs for any no-deal scenario. By that, I mean that the government had wanted to see a deal done by the autumn of 2018 and they had planned to write into the legislation that deadline to make MPs focus down. But when the legislation was finally agreed they moved the deadline to mid-January 2019, which became the new date that businesses would focus on. They were giving themselves as much time as possible to secure a deal with the EU and to get UK MPs onside, but they were allowing very little time for MPs to actually agree to the negotiations before 29 March 2019 when Article 50 would take effect. It looked like they were attempting to place MPs in a corner and give them no time to do anything other than approve the deal with the EU. It seemed to me that the timescales would be very tight and that the government might be planning to extend the Article 50 deadline out further beyond 29 March.

We started recording the show. It's a very informal style and all the presenters and guests merrily 'crash' into each other all the time. But the team put me at ease, and through all the laughter and political banter I was able to make an early point: 'The timescale keeps pushing further out. Keep September to November totally clear for the negotiations and the deadline keeps moving back,' I said. 'I am starting to hear a whisper about the UK government asking for an extension to the negotiations.' BBC Europe editor Katya Adler agreed. She told listeners: 'I am hearing the EU planning for the same kind of extension.'

I also said that in a very *sotto voce* way, business was being told by government and the No. 10 machine that it was aiming for the softest Brexit possible. Laura Kuenssberg smiled – she knew that Tory MPs and especially ERG MPs were being told something very different.

14

'F**K BUSINESS'

If Mansion House was the high-water mark of Theresa May's Brexit strategy, it may also have proved to be the high tide on her ability to align business and political leaders in the post-referendum environment. After that point, either her Cabinet fought her or business felt betrayed on the commitments it believed had been secured. Never again under May's premiership were we to see willing cooperation across all sides of the debate. That coalition was lost.

The run-up to the infamous Chequers meeting was perhaps the most frustrating period for industry since the 2016 vote. Business believed the Cabinet had alighted on a plan, delivered at Mansion House, that would provide a meaningful pathway towards the negotiation of the future relations with the EU. But the most important – and immediate – need for most business leaders was to secure the exit deal and therefore transition. By late April 2018 the Cabinet had set off on a fractious argument about the future relationship and the settlement around goods being traded across the Northern Ireland border, in particular. But, practically, the clamour I heard from our economic leaders at the time was to secure the exit deal first: secure the transition.

One senior FTSE chairman told me in early June 2018:

> The Cabinet is clearly losing the plot and has lost sight of the prize. When I negotiate, I do things one step at a time. Right now, the Cabinet does not seem to have an earthly clue of what they are doing, and the Prime Minister does not have the political authority to push forward.

This was certainly true. While Theresa May had secured an agreement at the March EU summit which built on the UK commitment to the Northern Ireland 'backstop' signed in December 2017, her Cabinet was all at sea. In late May 2018, one Cabinet member said to me:

> We are going round and round in ever decreasing circles. I can't tell you what is in the PM's mind. That's the way she likes it, but it is driving everyone crazy, destroying trust around the table, and I don't think that it is going to be possible to keep everyone on board around Cabinet.

As usual, I fed back this intelligence to business. I wish I could say anyone was really surprised. So now – with less than a year to go before the planned EU exit date – I saw business begin to spend a fortune on its planning and rewiring. There was no time to waste. Overall, the amount spent on Brexit has been truly eye-watering. According to analysis cited by the spring of 2019, after the planned exit day, the UK's ten largest domestic and foreign banks have spent over

£1 billion on their Brexit rewiring plans, with much of that spend taking place during 2018 as the politicians in the UK and the EU kept missing their own deadlines.

Across the wider economy there were some other notable numbers from important UK businesses: AstraZeneca reportedly spent $40 million on its rewiring, which would have been enough for ten clinical trials to be launched; insurer HISCOX spent around $15 million – enough to cover about 340 flood claim pay-outs; and EasyJet spent around £9 million – that's 9,836 flights of lost earnings.[30] In fact, EasyJet's reported results in spring 2019 showed the impact the economic uncertainty was having on the sector. For example, in May 2019, the company reported that its shares had fallen 13 per cent since its April trading update, to their lowest in more than two years.[31] Other airlines reported that they had seen a significant fall in bookings as a result of the uncertainty caused by the political vacillation.

Fast-forward to 16 May 2019, when I was writing my regular notes for *The Times*. Policy editor Oliver Wright and his lobby colleague Henry Zeffman have kindly provided me with a regular column to talk about business and Brexit throughout the negotiations. On the day that Theresa May made clear to the backbench 1922 Committee that she would be stepping down in June 2019 after having failed to get her deal passed, I wrote:

> Every pound spent on the rewiring is not being spent on growth or opportunities. While the management

---

30 Joe Mayes, 'What Brexit Will Cost Some of Britain's Leading Companies', Bloomberg, 12 April 2019.

31 Sky News, 'EasyJet bookings hit by Brexit and economic uncertainty', 17 May 2019.

consultants and lawyers have done well, our politics has not done well for our businesses. Deal. No deal. Many now don't care. They have spent the money.[32]

But back in June 2018 I was to put pen to electronic paper to create what was perhaps the most eye-catching thing I had ever written. It was designed to be. It was a response to another eye-catching comment by then Foreign Secretary Boris Johnson, who – admittedly frustrated by the entire government approach towards Brexit and the ongoing lobbying from business groups in particular – had snorted: 'F**k business' (albeit in a private diplomatic setting). Johnson had been intensely involved in the increasingly fractious Cabinet discussions about the trading arrangements across the Northern Ireland border. Around that time, the government had been hosting a major diplomatic event at Lancaster House in London. He had spent the evening being harangued by diplomatic and business leaders who kept asking him about business concerns over Brexit. After the incessant questions he just let rip. It appears the Belgian Ambassador, who overheard Johnson, decided to break diplomatic protocol and tell the newspapers – who then had a field day.

I was spending time away from politics to celebrate my husband's birthday weekend. When I opened the Sunday newspapers, 'F**k Business' was the dominant headline. It was the day that England played Panama in the World Cup. I knew I wanted to watch the match, but their story about Boris's comments needed a response. I awaited a denial or

---

32 Iain Anderson, 'Deal or no deal, businesses don't care', *The Times*, 16 May 2019.

a statement from his team which would have retracted or at least added context to the remark, but there was very little being said. It was only a few days later that he let it be known through others that he had been talking about the business organisations and the lobbyists. When launching his leadership bid to be Prime Minister one year later in June 2019, Johnson said: 'If sometimes ... I use phrases and language which have caused offence, I, of course, am sorry for the offence I have caused. But I will continue to speak as directly as I can because that is what I think the British public want.'

I knew why Boris had said it. Everyone had grown tired of the debate by then. He also was clearly about to grow tired of the constant pivoting around from No. 10 attempting to be all things at once to Leavers and Remainers in Cabinet. We were all tired of it. The pivoting was to continue all the way into 2019 in order the mask the true divide in the Cabinet and in the Conservative Party on the way ahead. The business 'lobby' had never been on his side since he abandoned David Cameron. It had been a remarkable turnaround from his time as Mayor of London where he had been the most pro-business Mayor in the job since it was created. Major global corporates flocked to his side and wanted him to be on their speaking roster for the World Economic Forum at Davos. But the referendum had changed everything. We had known him to be pro-enterprise before 2016, but at that moment the trenches between Boris and business leaders were just too deep. Words matter more in politics than in any other profession besides the law. At that moment the gap widened.

It was also an attack on lobbying or at least some of the

more prominent business lobby groups. At the time Francis Ingham, head of the Public Relations and Communications Association, told the Total Politics website: '[If Johnson was referring to lobbyists] that would mean that one of the most senior people in the government said "f**k lobbyists" – in itself an insulting and outrageous sentiment. Lobbying plays a vital role in our democracy.'[33]

Speaking to me for this book, David Frost – one of Boris's special advisers while he was Foreign Secretary and who was to join him in Downing Street in late July 2019 as his chief EU adviser – told me:

> Boris was surrounded by people in this tent at Lancaster House. It was very hot and absolutely rammed. He kept being asked about Brexit – 'Why are you doing this? Why are you doing this? Business doesn't like it.' He kind of snapped. There was a lot of pressure at the time in the run-up to Chequers. But it absolutely does not represent his view of business, as he has since made very clear.

I sat down to watch the England match, but I was itching to write. I bashed out my *Times* column over the first half of the game in record time. As England was punishing Panama to a 6–1 drubbing, the words flowed rather excitedly. Before the game was over, I sent it to Zeffman. Given the title of this book, let me reprise it here in full:

---

33 David Singleton, 'Robert Halfon explains all about Boris Johnson's "f*** business" outburst', Total Politics, 25 June 2018.

BUSINESS HAS SPOKEN – BORIS JOHNSON, IT'S TIME TO GO

This Brexit business is a really exhausting business. And business itself is now really exhausted by it. And particularly exhausted by the ongoing destructive position of Her Britannic Majesty's secretary of state for foreign affairs. This weekend the most important business groups in our country – representing large and small firms alike – wrote to the prime minister; Jean-Claude Juncker, the European Commission president; and Donald Tusk, president of the European Council, outlining their deep concerns on the trajectory of Brexit negotiations and the future of pan European supply chains and passporting for our service industries that make up 80 per cent of our GDP.

In response to these legitimate and thoughtful concerns this month our foreign secretary is reported to have snorted: 'F**k business'. Is that really what our foreign secretary thinks in his private moments? Really? Really?

Put simply, it is not for the government to dismiss the concerns of business. We do not – thankfully – live in a country where the government is our main employer. The role of government is to create the platform on which businesses, both global and domestic, flourish. Government policy and regulation is merely a framework.

That any Cabinet minister in this country would dismiss the concerns of business in four crass letters shows someone unable to see that a Brexit that works requires flexibility on all sides.

As I write this piece I have yet to hear Boris Johnson or his entourage repudiate such an offensive remark.

The tragedy is this is not some Oxbridge debating society parlour game. It's rather more serious. It's about the future of our country and it's about having a civilised discourse with the government and knowing those at the top of Whitehall really care about our economy. I'm not sure expletives convince me of that.

Unfortunately for too many politicians this means that the difficult decisions that business leaders need to take about employing people or where the next deal or order is coming from might not have troubled them too much throughout their life.

These decisions are, however, central to the livelihoods of millions of Britons and indeed the economic future of our nation.

For too long commerce has been promised the 'best' Brexit. However, in the last week I was told by a government official that the best we could hope for is to be the 'best third country'. Nothing very 'deep' or 'special' about that.

So that appears to be the aim for the Chequers summit in July to sort out the final UK negotiating position for our future relationship – not quite the idea the government seemed to have in mind after the last Chequers summit in March that led to the prime minister's pragmatic Mansion House speech.

Theresa May is actually doing an amazing job tenaciously trying to secure a Brexit despite the foreign secretary's efforts.

The reasons Airbus, BMW, Siemens and our dominant service sector are breaking cover now is that they have to make plans to satisfy their customers and their shareholders.

Business is not making empty threats – believe me, I know that. They are already moving supply chains and people.

Last month the foreign secretary is reported to have asked for public spending on a 'Boris Force One' to tour the world 'drumming up business'. Mr Johnson would do well to stay grounded in the UK, focused on keeping the fantastic global businesses we have in the country.

The real tragedy is that Mr Johnson was a tremendous asset for our country while he was the mayor of London and was great at promoting our business prospects around the world. Now I know no company who willingly wants him on their platform.

As foreign secretary he is not doing business any favours, he is not doing the prime minister or her government any favours and he is not doing the process of Brexit any favours.

Mr Johnson's reported dismissal of business concerns raises serious questions if he is a politician who really has the interests of the nation at heart. It appears Michael Gove's misgivings about him were spot on in the summer of 2016 – imagine the impact of Bojo as prime minister right now. I have no doubt capital would be in flight if he was leading negotiations.

I spend my time focused on keeping business here in the UK and aiming to make Britain adopt policies as the best country in the world to do business.

I wish the foreign secretary would do the same. But I've

had enough. If Mr Johnson has used such words about business we need a new foreign secretary batting for British interests.

It's time for Boris to go.

Well, the words created waves. Zeffman texted me back and said: 'We will turn this into a news piece as well.' When my column appeared the next morning and Zeffman wrote his news item I had a mix of calls and messages from the political and the business world applauding the sentiments. But the most interesting message came from inside No. 10 itself. I got a WhatsApp note saying: 'Thank god you said that – because we can't.'

However, within days businesses had calmed down from Boris's words. For most, they hadn't really registered at all. Recalling his thoughts at the time, former Barclays chair John McFarlane told me: 'While Boris used the "F" word – he really is pro-business. I know he is pro-business from his time as London mayor and I was on the board of Westfield [the shopping centre property developer].'

Martin Gilbert – another City heavyweight – agrees. He said: 'When Boris said "F**k business" I just totally disregarded it. It was Boris being Boris. He is more serious than that and I actually think he likes business.'

Boris Johnson's words were a remarkable admission from the heart of government, but it was to be the foretaste of the months of debate to come. The Prime Minister had no grip on her most senior ministers. The frustration was endless. In many ways, Johnson was right to call it out. By the end of that week, my call for Boris to go had caught fire on the

Times Red Box site as the most-read column of the week, in a frenzied atmosphere in the final run-up to the Chequers meeting. While businesses were frustrated that the Brexit negotiation was stuck, the mood music coming towards the City was that the Mansion House approach still worked and was being negotiated with the EU. The CEO of one of the banks told me: 'We were being told right up until the last moment before Chequers by the Treasury that we would see the government reaffirm its commitment to mutual recognition at Chequers.'

On Friday 6 July, the Cabinet gathered at the Prime Minister's Buckinghamshire residence to thrash out the approach to the next stage of the negotiations. The Prime Minister had already been defeated in the Cabinet sub-committee, which had been looking at the Northern Ireland border arrangements, with a majority of Cabinet members voting for the max fac option. This was the so-called maximum facilitation approach, which meant that customs declaration and clearance procedures would take place in advance, away from the border, and surveillance would be intelligence-led, rather than old-fashioned random searches. But in the intense heat of the summer of 2018, the tensions in the Cabinet seemed to boil over when they decided to continue discussions outside.

By mid-evening the details of the agreement had leaked, and my team forwarded them on to major businesses and some of the business organisations. In the end there were just two small paragraphs on services – reflecting 80 per cent of the UK economy. While there was to be more in a subsequent White Paper a week later, services looked on in horror. What had appeared was not what had been promised. It looked like mutual recognition for services – still promised by the government only days before the Cabinet met – had been dropped in favour of equivalence. Let's look at what the UK government White Paper set out the following week. On financial services, it called for:

- A new economic and regulatory arrangement with the EU in financial services. The government suggests this would maintain the economic benefits of cross-border provision between the UK and the EU, preserving regulatory and supervisory cooperation, financial stability, market integrity and consumer protection.
- This new economic and regulatory arrangement would be based on the principle of autonomy for each party over decisions regarding access to its market, with a bilateral framework of treaty-based commitments to underpin the operation of the relationship, ensure transparency and stability, and promote cooperation.
- However, such an arrangement would respect the regulatory autonomy of both parties, while ensuring decisions made by either party are implemented in line with agreed processes.
- The existing autonomous frameworks for equivalence would need to be expanded, to reflect the fact that equivalence as it exists today is not sufficient in scope for the breadth of the interconnectedness of UK–EU financial services provision.
- The new arrangement would need to encompass a broader range of cross-border activities that reflect global financial business models and the high degree of economic integration.

- However, this arrangement cannot replicate the EU's passporting regime.
- The UK proposes that there should be reciprocal recognition of equivalence under all existing third country regimes, taking effect at the end of the implementation period.

But the White Paper spent much more time on goods than services, and proposed alignment:

- The government proposes a common rulebook for goods, including agri-food, covering only those rules necessary to provide for frictionless trade at the border. This means the government must make an upfront choice to commit by treaty to ongoing harmonisation with the relevant EU rules. The common rulebook will be legislated for in the UK Parliament and the devolved legislatures. The UK will also seek participation – as an active participant, albeit without voting rights – in EU technical committees that have a role in designing and implementing rules that form part of the common rulebook.
- The government also proposes a common rulebook for state aid, establishing cooperative agreements between regulators on competition, and agreeing to maintain high standards through non-regression provisions in areas including the environment and employment rules.
- The joint institutional arrangements proposed will ensure that in areas where the government is proposing the UK would remain party to a common rulebook, there will be a clear process for updating relevant rules. It will also ensure that both the UK and the EU interpret rules consistently.

Finally, on customs and free trade, the White Paper said:

- The government reiterates the Chequers agreement in stating that the UK and EU should focus on ensuring the continuation of frictionless and reciprocal market access for goods through the establishment of a free trade area, albeit not covering services. This is in order to protect the integrated supply chains and 'just-in-time' processes that are currently in place, whilst respecting the 'integrity' of the EU's single market, customs union and rules-based framework. It also commits the government to being able to forge new trade relationships with third countries.

Broadly, the economic partnership includes:

- A common rulebook for manufactured, agriculture, food and fisheries goods, only going so far as to cover those rules necessary to maintaining frictionless trade at the border between the UK and EU. As part of this arrange-ment, the UK will also seek continued participation in EU agencies that facilitate goods entering the EU market.
- A phased introduction of a new Facilitated Customs Ar-rangement that would remove the need for customs checks and controls between the UK and the EU as if they were in a combined customs territory and enabling the UK to set its own tariffs for trade with third countries.
- A market surveillance framework to ensure rules are upheld in both markets.
- A commitment to no tariffs on any goods, a common rulebook for state aid, the establishment of cooperative

arrangements between regulators on competition, and an agreement to maintain high standards in areas such as environment and employment rules.[34]

Back on 6 July, when details of the Chequers agreement began to leak out, TheCityUK bashed out a statement, saying: 'Mutual recognition would have been the best way forward. It is therefore regrettable and frustrating that this approach has been dropped before even making it to the negotiating table.'

While David Davis and Boris Johnson climbed into their ministerial cars (the Cabinet had been told they would have to summon a local taxi firm if they resigned and walked out of the meeting there and then) it would be less than forty-eight hours later before ministers started to resign. DExEU ministers David Davis and Steve Baker would quit in time for the late-night news on Sunday 8 July; overnight I could not resist a tweet calling them 'DExEU's midnight runners'. Matt Chorley – Red Box editor at *The Times* – was delighted and featured it in his well-read morning email update. It summed up the rather darkly comic mood of the time, perhaps.

Holed up all of Monday in his official Foreign and Commonwealth Office grace-and-favour home in Carlton Gardens, Boris Johnson was to resign by mid-afternoon. Little did I think that less than two weeks after writing my column, Boris would indeed have to go – albeit at a time (broadly) of his own choosing. In his resignation letter, Johnson said: 'We have postponed crucial decisions ... with the result that we

---

34 'The future relationship between the United Kingdom and the European Union', Department for Exiting the European Union, July 2018.

appear to be heading for a semi-Brexit, with large parts of our economy still locked in the EU system, but with no UK control over that system.'[35] Of course, in many ways he was exactly right. But for the City, the opposite was true; financial services might be locked out of the new arrangements.

In many ways it was remarkable that May had kept her Foreign Secretary and Brexit Secretary for so long, given the clear tensions about her approach, but Chequers was one of those moments in the whole Brexit drama where cans could no longer be kicked down the road. It was decision time and a turning point in the future of the May government. The politicians were unhappy. Businesses were unhappy. The EU Commission appeared unhappy and Parliament was soon to become very unhappy. Given how many services businesses were feeling after Chequers, 'business has been f**ked' might have been a more accurate sentiment. Speaking to me for this book, one Cabinet minister who stayed around the table and later backed Boris Johnson for the Tory leadership told me: 'I would not have used the expression "F**k business". We should be saying "F**k government".'

---

35 'Boris Johnson's resignation letter and May's reply in full', BBC News, 9 July 2018.

15

WITHDRAWING FROM THE WITHDRAWAL PLAN

Within days of Chequers, the business lobbying had started in earnest yet again. The White Paper written by civil servants, outlining in some depth the ambitions for the UK's post-Brexit relationship, which had replaced the short statement agreed by the Cabinet, hailed a new 'economic partnership' with the EU, but all business could see was an intention to be aligned with the EU single market for goods in order to get around the Northern Ireland border issues and to be the 'best third country' for services. The David Davis idea of a 'mini union' with the EU had been killed off.

With Davis sweeping himself away from government, business and EU Commissioner Michel Barnier had a new interlocutor in freshly appointed DExEU Secretary Dominic Raab. Business had never really warmed to Davis during his tenure in the role. Admittedly, the breezy self-confidence he had always displayed that Brexit would be 'all right on the night' for the economy had been replaced with rather more detailed economic thinking from his ever-expanding department. Raab was less of a known quantity for the business lobby, but the fact that he – as one of the leading lights of the Leave campaign – had signed up to the Chequers plan, gave industry some sense that the government could hold it together on the approach.

Brussels was rather more sceptical about Chequers. Unlike the welcoming tone from EU Brexit Commissioner Michel Barnier towards Mansion House, the EU Commission viewed this more detailed roadmap for the talks as a direct attack on the 'integrity' of EU membership, with Theresa May 'cherry picking' between single market alignment for goods and equivalence for services. The initial response from Barnier was cautious, with the negotiator remarking on the UK proposals on customs: 'How could we avoid that an autonomous British commercial policy, while keeping all the advantages of our customs union, offers British companies major competitive advantages, to the detriment of EU companies?'[36]

Business in the UK was not unduly concerned about the initial Brussels riposte. This was a negotiation starting point for both sides. It was the most detailed explanation of the UK's views since the referendum – of course the other side would greet it in this way. Most businesspeople knew that negotiation worked that way (or negotiations should work that way at least). You start with a maximalist position on both sides and you give yourself enough wiggle room to draw to a deal. May's problem, of course, was that she wasn't just negotiating with the EU Commission – she was also

---

36 Michel Barnier, 'Press statement following the July 2018 General Affairs Council (Article 50)', 20 July 2018.

negotiating with her own Cabinet and the UK Parliament throughout the process.

Just days after Chequers, No. 10 filled a position which had been left vacant for over a year: the head of business relations. The vacancy had proven hard to fill. In fact, in the spring of 2018, I had taken a call from a former No. 10 insider and leader of one of the UK's foremost business groups asking me if I knew anyone who might want to apply for the role. I gave them my thoughts, but it took another five months to hire someone. For the first year of May's government, from 2016 to 2017, antipathy to business was clear. For the second full year, there was no senior figure in Downing Street leading business relations. Of course, this was not necessarily a job that was easy to sell. Because of the approach taken by the government, no senior business figure would believe that the role would be given the clout needed to make it work. Further, given the precarious nature of the May regime after the 2017 election, no one knew how long the job would last.

Nikki da Costa, who served as director of legislative affairs in Downing Street from the summer of 2017 until she resigned in November 2018, joined Cicero in January 2019. Nikki went back to No. 10 in the same role in July 2019 to be part of Boris Johnson's new government. She told me: 'I was continually arguing that we needed the business team to be part of the decision-making process at the highest level throughout my time in Downing Street. But under May there just appeared to be a blind spot on all this.'

William Vereker was appointed as business envoy and took up his post on 3 September 2018. An investment banker by trade, he arrived from UBS. He had spent thirty years in the City, including stints at Morgan Stanley, Lehman Brothers and Nomura, with an early specialism in banking for the energy and power sectors. The *Financial Times* reported his appointment in late July 2018, saying:

> He had been seeking an exit after he was moved sideways last year from his role running UBS's global investment banking division into the less prestigious post of 'executive vice-chair'. He privately backed leaving the EU during the 2016 referendum and is understood to have strong views on British sovereignty and immigration.

Vereker did set out to refresh business relations and 'open the door' to Downing Street and to the rest of government towards business. Within weeks his fresh approach was to become evident as Downing Street hosted a rolling series of briefings for business leaders and introduced frequent conference calls with ministers to better inform business about what was actually going on. I will reflect on those meetings a little later.

By the time business leaders gathered in Birmingham in early October for the Tory Party conference, a new mood had overtaken them. Six months on from Mansion House and almost three months on from Chequers, they had the overriding sense that the sand was running out on the Article 50 timer. The government continued to tell voters that the UK would be leaving the EU on 29 March 2019 at 11 p.m., but no one knew if that would be with a transitional period and a deal on the future relationship. The intensity of the Brexit rewiring from business would reach new heights. There really was no time to waste, but government could give business no guarantees at all. Everyone who could implement their plans was doing just that.

The expression I had started to hear most often from my clients by the time of the Tory conference was that transition was a 'withering asset'. What did that mean? Most businesses still wanted to see a transition period, but the realities of the ticking clock meant that they were faced with major strategic choices which could not be left to chance. The single market passport was not on offer in any way. There was no guarantee that the Prime Minister's approach would work either in Brussels or inside the UK Parliament, where she was also negotiating for political headroom. Perhaps it would just be for the best to continue to assume that no deal and therefore no transition would be secured.

The Cicero dinner at the 2018 Tory conference was the biggest we had ever hosted. Our acquisition of Westbourne had catapulted our brand awareness and our reach across the UK's key economic sectors. A range of players from our core base of financial services were in the room but they were there alongside tech, infrastructure, digital, housing and transport businesses. Our party conference dinner has become a real highlight of my business year. It is an opportunity to stand back from the conference goldfish bowl and relax a little. It was also a great opportunity to allow business to rub shoulders with the Westminster 'bubble' that descends now on Birmingham, Manchester and Brighton. On the Monday night we gathered at the Birmingham Hotel du Vin for drinks and a bite to eat. I had asked a range of commentators to join us to provide clients with their latest thinking on the politics. Former Sky News deputy political editor and Theresa May spokesman Joey Jones had just joined Cicero as our senior political counsel. I had got to know Joey when he was at Sky and we had met a few times, most notably in Brussels in the early 2010s during one of the endless eurozone crisis summits. We had kept in touch and I was delighted to bring him to Cicero to support the development of our business with his superb political nous and presentation skills. I asked him to chair proceedings that night at our dinner. For the first time since we launched the business, I was able to sit back and totally enjoy the evening without the need to be performing.

City AM editor Christian May gave our guests an insight into the need for the Tories to get behind the Prime Minister's approach, otherwise the prospect of Corbyn would loom larger on the horizon for business than ever before. *The Times*'s Oliver Wright talked of the travails inside government and continued to point to his namesake Olly Robbins as the person with the tightest grip on the negotiations. Columnist Ayesha Hazarika gave us her inimitable tour de force left-of-centre peek into the Tory proceedings and what Labour might do in response in the months ahead.

Our government speaker, solicitor general Robert Buckland, stayed religiously on message, calling for Tories to get behind the Prime Minister or face a political crisis. Buckland had been praised for single-handedly keeping the Brexit legislation on track in the House of Commons earlier that year when he was being assailed by both the ERG and Labour simultaneously. Buckland later confided to me over that dinner that the government whips were considering offering

Tory MPs a 'free vote' on any confirmatory vote on the final Brexit deal. The idea was that, without whipping on either side, MPs would be faced with the reality of that ticking clock and would come to their senses. Of course, the idea was never to come to pass, but it gives an insight into how fragile the government was – and the No. 10 and whipping 'strategy' – even before the turn of 2018 into the calamitous events of the first half of 2019. When a final history of Brexit is written, Buckland's role behind the scenes in keeping the legislation afloat under both the May and Johnson administrations will prove to have been crucial.

The next day I met up with Nikki da Costa in the main conference hotel and we talked about the parliamentary votes ahead. Nikki was already anticipating a tortuous passage for the legislation and was gaming every twist and turn in a delayed process in the House of Commons which was likely to take us to the wire on 29 March. She told me at the time: 'It's already looking very tight but MPs are going to have to wake up and decide whether they want to let Brexit happen and therefore transition happen – or not.'

The next month of British and EU politics in the run-up to the end of November proved to be the precursor to the most intense and exhausting time in my own business and political life. If I thought the previous two years had been melodramatic, this was as nothing compared to the Westminster machinations ahead. I had never known a period when businesses were so fixated on the political ins and outs on whether or not the UK would secure a deal with Brussels. Sterling had become the proxy for the likelihood of a deal or a no-deal. When the Cicero team sent out our latest briefing notes on the politics of the period to major investors, we knew they were being widely shared across the City, and both money and people were being moved on the basis of the political tempo.

In mid-November I was due in New York to brief investors on the unfolding politics. I had got on the plane in London on the evening of 13 November against a backdrop of a UK Cabinet once again fighting openly in the media with itself. Time to enjoy a few glasses of my favoured pinot noir on board and escape for a few hours. Being on a plane remains one of the few places that affords you thinking time, cut off from our digitised world. I am firmly resisting the option to connect to the inflight WiFi that is being rolled out on airlines for precisely that reason!

When I landed at JFK Airport late that evening, I was surprised to see the UK Cabinet still intact and all around the table. The next day I headed to brief a series of short- and long-term Wall Street investors with a big investment weighting into the UK. I saw a mix of traditional asset managers who invest over many years and the hedge funds who trade around economic and political events with op-portunism. The weather in New York was set to be as bleak as British politics. On that first day I was laying out Cicero's detailed unpacking of the politics when we had to stop the meetings and watch the Prime Minister walk onto the steps of Downing Street and tell the waiting cameras that she had secured a Cabinet deal to take to Brussels. I watched as some of the investors left the meeting room in midtown Manhat-tan in order to trade on the positive political news.

On the face of it, the UK Cabinet appeared to be in lockstep, but within moments it was reported that the Prime Minister had in fact locked up the Cabinet in Downing Street without their mobile phones to ensure they did not leak from the meeting before she got a chance to brief the media. Within the hour, the Cabinet were allowed to leave No. 10 and the counter-briefing against the meeting began in earnest. It all felt wearily like Chequers a few months before. I warned the Wall Street investors that day to continue to plan on the basis that securing a deal may only come at the last moment of the process.

I spent that evening relaxing away from Brexit while in New York at a fantastic dinner near Wall Street hosted by Suki Sandhu, founder of the business LGBT network OUT-standing. Sandhu has kindly highlighted my work for the SME sector and with politicians on supporting LGBT people in business at home and internationally, and provided brilliant mentoring opportunities. He had invited many of the other role models he has brought together over the last decade for the dinner. It is brilliant, uplifting work and, in the midst of the mess of our politics, something to genuinely celebrate. It was nice to spend time away from the subject and, psychologically, to focus on something that appeared to be moving forwards not backwards. I savoured the Californian red wine served at dinner and it transported me back to the American west coast and my dreams and hopes for the future.

Following this genuine celebration of business life, I went back to my hotel feeling considerably more upbeat than the political news should have allowed me to be. It would not last for long. The jet lag kicked in around 4 a.m. New York time and I woke bolt upright – but perhaps my body was also switching on its political antenna. Moments later Cicero UK public affairs director Tom Frackowiak sent me a text: 'Raab has resigned. Sorry to wake you up. Thought you might like to know about it.' I have had an uncanny knack for years to be able to wake up in the middle of the night for significant political events. I can go to sleep and almost know when to wake up for a minor by-election result around 3 a.m.! I know other political geeks who have the same capabilities. We are clearly hardwired for politics.

I got straight up and powered up my iPad to catch the latest UK updates. By now, other Cabinet members, including Work and Pension Secretary Esther McVey, were also stepping away from Theresa May and had resigned. The prospects of a deal and transition appeared more remote once again. I took to Twitter: 'Business is watching with horror the resignations now taking place. Yesterday we had stability and today we do not. There is now no time to renegotiate another deal. We thought we had stability – and now we have instability writ large #Brexit.' Then Sky News political editor Faisal Islam retweeted me with his comment: 'Vista from a well-connected Conservative link to biz community'.

Within minutes, I also got the news that Nikki da Costa had left Downing Street suddenly and would not be helping push the deal through Westminster. This was a major blow to the Prime Minister. Nikki had done more to keep the Brexit legislation flowing over the past year than even the chief whip. She knew the parliamentary party like the back of her hand and had helped navigate the Brexit machinations across Parliament. Her role was created specifically for her in the summer of 2017 in order for No. 10 to better manage relations with MPs, especially after Theresa May had lost her parliamentary majority. I texted her and said we must meet when I got back to London. She replied within minutes.

My subsequent four meetings in New York on 15 November with investors were to take on board a rather surreal quality. I had now ripped up my political presentation entirely and gave them all a running commentary on events in London. To get to the meetings I was trudging through a huge and suddenly falling New York snowstorm – the kind of snow that can only appear in Manhattan. It dumps down so rapidly and creates transport gridlock. In between meetings I was glued to my smartphone to comprehend the machinations in London.

The meetings in New York were now kept brief – I could tell the investors were heading out of the room to 'short' – or bet against – the pound yet again. But the focus of the conversation in that second day changed gear. Investors had heard enough about Brexit – they wanted to hear much more about the prospect of Jeremy Corbyn and John McDonnell being in Downing Street. They were assuming – rightly – that UK politics was so unstable that the prospects of a general election were significantly heightened. What would it mean for the UK? What would it mean for their long- and short-term investments in the UK? What would the Labour plan for business and investors look like? Might there be controls on the flow of capital in and out of the UK? Again, I could sense that Wall Street was becoming very risk-averse about the UK's political trajectory and, as the fund managers like to say, 'taking money off the table' – that's taking money away from the UK.

I then flew directly from New York to Milan to travel to my annual get-together with German policymakers and business leaders with the Konrad Adenauer Foundation. I had slept extremely well on the plane – rather exhausted by events and by having had a nightmarish journey to get out of Manhattan in the snow to JFK. The town was gridlocked. Usually when in New York I had hit my Uber app to hail a ride to the airport for an all-in cost of around $50; tonight it was indicating that Uber's surge pricing would take that fare to around $400! I grabbed my bags and trudged through the midtown snow to get to the subway and then on to Penn Station to get the Airtrain to JFK. I guessed that the train would be a better way through the snow that night. I was soon checking in for the Emirates flight to Milan.

My shoes were soggy from the walk in the snow and I was drenched by the weather, so I wanted a hot shower at the airport just to relax and to warm up. I then grabbed a meal in the terminal to be able to get straight to sleep on the plane. That feeling of nervous tension to get to an airport on time in bad weather and then sitting down relaxed on the plane with a drink in hand always makes me fall asleep with minutes. I sat on board the mighty Airbus 380 'Superjumbo' and was asleep straight after the flight safety video, before we even took off from New York.

I landed in Milan having slept for almost seven hours and we headed to Lake Como, where I went straight into delivering a speech on global trade prospects. Over the next two days the Brits and the Germans talked about the prospects for Brexit and everyone felt rather gloomy all together. KAS UK director Felix Dane had also asked me to be the after-dinner

speaker at the event on the following night. Having attended since the early 2010s, I had become something of an old
hand at the KAS retreat at Cadenabbia. I aimed to lift the
spirits, using the speech to remind us all of the friendships
we shared, and hoped for a deal at the EU summit ahead we
could all sign up to.

Despite the tortures of the previous few weeks, May did
secure her deal with EU leaders on 25 November 2018. By
then she had needed a new Brexit Secretary to help her sell
the deal. This time it was Steve Barclay. This was good for
business. As we saw during his tenure as City minister, Barclay remained a pragmatist and does to this day. Speaking to
me for this book he told me: 'It was a strange moment. When
I arrived, the deal had been all but written. I was charged
with going out to sell it, of course, but I had had no input to
the approach beforehand.'

Now a deal was done with the EU, it was time to sell the
deal to Tory MPs, the DUP, some Labour MPs and to business. By now Vereker had been in Downing Street for just
over three months and I was invited along with around a
hundred business leaders to attend a reception in Downing
Street in November 2018 to hear from the Prime Minister
about 'her' deal. It was instructive to note that all her Cabinet ministers were already referring to the UK government's
signed deal with the EU as the 'Prime Minister's deal'. Even
her Chancellor Philip Hammond and Business Secretary
Greg Clark – the two ministers who would be closest to her
in the approach – would use that terminology. It was almost
as if the Cabinet believed that they could distance themselves from it. As I have discussed throughout this book, the

principle of 'collective responsibility' seemed to be well and truly dead – maybe it had died back in February 2016 when David Cameron allowed Cabinet ministers to campaign on either side of the referendum itself. The grip of power for Cameron weakened from that moment and it was there for all to see throughout the May years.

As I arrived in No. 10, I mingled over soft drinks with the other leaders, spotting John McFarlane and Santander chair Shriti Vadera. We walked into the Downing Street state dining room and sat next to each other for the briefing from the Cabinet. Everyone entering the room was to be greeted personally by the Chancellor; the red carpet was being rolled out for Britain's corporate top dogs. The government wanted us to sell the deal and to help to convince MPs too.

William Vereker welcomed everyone to the room and introduced Steve Barclay to set the scene. In the job little over a week, Barclay was as impressive as ever, but he quickly handed over to the Prime Minister's chief of staff, Gavin Barwell, who proceeded to take us through a densely populated PowerPoint presentation. It was clear to me that, alongside Olly Robbins, the deal was being owned by Barwell too. He was all over the detail and spoke with some passion. He appeared to have more of a grip on the detail than many of the Cabinet. It was instructive: the deal had been baked in Downing Street by Downing Street, and No. 10 was taking full ownership of proceedings. It reminded me of David Cameron's approach to his own renegotiation in early 2016. Theresa May would now be front and central to the sales pitch to MPs and the nation.

Around this time – before and after the Downing Street

reception – the chatter among business leaders and MPs became: 'Did you get PowerPointed by No. 10?' The deal presentation was an overly long deck of slides which were talked through at high pace. Of course, the detail was complicated – necessarily so – but it seemed to me that most MPs' attention would wander if presented with this dense deck with little time to digest each page. PowerPoint was also becoming a really outdated way of making an argument in modern business life, as it has become clear that the emotional connection is often lost between a speaker and their audience because those listening try to watch the speaker and simultaneously read the words on screen. There is no surprise that many business organisations have binned the use of PowerPoint. It is often described as 'death by PowerPoint'. I had ceased to use the format years ago, as the moment I wrote down the words, the political landscape changed before my very eyes!

Sure enough, midway through the presentation McFarlane, Vadera and I started to glaze over with its message complexity. It was clear to me that this deck would be a hard sell to MPs, who often zone out within minutes if you don't engage them emotionally in an argument that will work for them, their constituency or their philosophy.

To end the presentation, the Prime Minister came into the room. She had been elsewhere in Downing Street that night, briefing or selling to Labour MPs who might be willing to back the deal. I knew my former Cicero colleague Joe Moor – then acting director of legislative affairs in Downing Street – would have been deeply involved in the targeting of those likely Labour MPs. Moor had joined Nikki da Costa in Downing Street in early 2018 and was now working hand in hand with Barwell to reach out across the Commons to try and sell the deal.

The Prime Minister had made a much simpler pitch without the horrors of PowerPoint. She wanted all of us in the room to go out and sell the deal to MPs across the country, to talk about her belief that the reality was that this was the only deal that would be on offer from the EU and to talk about the economic consequences of no deal. It was at this point that the strategy towards a soft Brexit I had discerned way back in the autumn of 2016 was actually uttered for the first time publicly by the Prime Minister. For many businesses in the room there was no great enthusiasm for the deal itself. It did not really have anything other than an ambition for the dominant services part of the UK economy – but the deal did secure transition. By the end of 2018, that's all business really wanted to know.

After the Prime Minister spoke, she took questions chaired by Vereker. I put my hand up late into the session and out of the corner of my eye I caught Jimmy McLoughlin, who was directing the field of questions from the back of the room, point Vereker to me. I asked the Prime Minister a simple question: 'Many of us feel bruised by backing Remain in 2016 – by making the economic case back then, how do we convince MPs now that they should back a deal backed by business?'

The Prime Minister paused, looked me straight in the eye and said: 'I know it's difficult, but everyone here has a responsibility to help secure transition and get a good deal for our country. We need you to tell our MPs just that. You employ people and your voices need to be heard.' You had to admire her straight talking and I felt most people in the room lean towards the Prime Minister for the first time since she had entered Downing Street, as they knew how complex and difficult the political journey had been. However, many in the room thought this effort would be a thankless task.

The Prime Minister left the room and everyone was invited to stay to have a glass of wine. I said hello to Steve Barclay and asked him if he was enjoying his new role. He smiled: 'It's certainly interesting.' I also bumped into British Chamber of Commerce director general Adam Marshall, who was very concerned about the time left to secure the deal with MPs and then the EU. But, as I looked around the rest of the room, I only saw another twenty faces remain behind for that drink. Despite being invited to have time with the Cabinet in No. 10, most of the 100 business leaders had headed straight for the door. Their rapid departure spoke volumes. In the days of Blair, Brown and Cameron, I had seen business leaders being poured out of No. 10 receptions late into the evening; not this time. Treasury Select Committee chair Nicky Morgan told me: 'Business started off in 2016 really caring about the outcome. By the end of 2018 many were saying they just wanted it all to be done and over with.'

In May 2019, reflecting on events, Barclay said: 'Politically this has been done all the wrong way around – it has been too late to do the deal.' He was pointing me back to the approach which Cameron and Oliver Letwin had offered in the small hours after the Brexit vote itself. The negotiations with Parliament – certainly inside the Tory Party and the DUP – should have started much earlier.

16

QUESTIONED TIMES

The end of 2018 saw a remarkable alignment between business and voters, in terms of sentiment at least. Politics was
clearly failing all of us. Everyone was sick of the stalemate at
Westminster, but the distance between those with economic
power and those without had never been greater in terms
of readiness. Our major businesses were getting themselves
sorted for Brexit. Smaller businesses didn't have that kind of
firepower and could only cross their fingers and hope that
the politicians could work out their differences.

December 2018 was utterly dismal. The Prime Minister
had planned to hold a vote on her Withdrawal Agreement
on 10 December after a week of parliamentary debate. The
day of the vote, Environment Secretary Michael Gove had
appeared on the BBC *Today* programme and confirmed that
the vote was to take place, only to find before lunchtime on
the same day that the vote had been pulled. It would take
another four weeks for Parliament to have the chance to vote
for the first time on the deal. For business, the government's
left and right hands didn't appear to know what they were
doing.

I have been used to watching politicians make last-minute decisions and trying to explain to businesses the delicate political calculations that governments have to make, but this move really took the biscuit. On the most important issue of the day – the only issue that government and Parliament was actually able to focus on – there would be no vote. For businesses attempting to decipher the madness of the situation, there was only one conclusion to make: that Tory chief whip Julian Smith was unable to guarantee that the Prime Minister's deal would pass the House of Commons. And he was right to do so.

Just two days later, Theresa May faced a Tory MPs vote of confidence pushed by the ERG. I appeared on talkRADIO the night of the vote to natter with political commentator Daisy McAndrew and their incisive political editor Ross Kempsell. I said that May needed to win at least 200 of her MPs to be safe for another year as leader under the current rules. Now, I hadn't written down the number 200 inside an envelope, but May won over exactly 200 of her MPs that night. That was to prove to be one of my most accurate calls – I should have taken a bet that night!

The festive break at the end of 2018 reminded me of Christmas a decade earlier. Then, exhaustion had set in after over a year of financial markets in turmoil. Consumers and companies felt more brittle than ever. There was a longing for some good news in the political air. There was little in prospect. Business just switched off over the break like the rest of Britain. It was good to stop talking about the 'B' word. The country felt as if it was trapped in a maze of our own making. Deborah Mattinson, the BritainThinks pollster, provided me with data to show that voters – both Leavers and Remainers – were concerned about their own mental health and that of their family and friends as a result of the ongoing paralysis in the country. I had wondered about my own at that time too. In just a few weeks, I was to discuss this on national television.

As a new year beckoned, I received a text from Andrew Bowie, the Aberdeenshire West and Kincardine MP who had become a firm friend since he entered Parliament. He told me he had been appointed as the Prime Minister's new PPS. After less than two years in Parliament, Bowie was already being marked out by the Tory whips as 'one to watch'. The whips were right to do so. Bowie's energy and enthusiasm were in marked contrast to most Tory MPs who spent their time simmering and backbiting over the period. One of the newly elected Scots Tories, his enthusiasm was infectious and free of the cynicism of times. But Bowie was nervous too. It would be a big job at the most momentous of times. Informally, I offered him the opportunity to feed business sentiment directly into the No. 10 machine.

Bowie knew what the rest of us did, that the Prime Minister would have to introduce her deal into Parliament before the end of January 2019. The legislation passed over the summer of 2018 made clear that the government would only be able to keep control of the timetable and not risk back-benchers taking control of the parliamentary order paper if they passed the deal that month. As I have discussed, in 2018 Parliament had passed legislation that provided a backstop date to the negotiations to be approved by the Commons and the Lords before the middle of January 2019.

On 15 January – after being delayed as long as politically possible to try to force Tory MPs, in particular, to back down – the government pushed ahead with the vote. It was a moment of the highest drama. All Westminster watchers knew when the opposition tellers walked down on the right-hand side of the Chamber with the result in their hands that the government had been defeated. It is the winning whips that always read out the result. But the scale of the defeat – the largest ever of a UK government in any parliament – broke the political dial – I think the Cicero 'Brexometer' cracked too at that point. It needed some explaining to business. What would the government do next? What could it do?

William Vereker – the new No. 10 business envoy – had by now firmly instituted his new way of talking to business leaders by introducing conference calls with Cabinet members to explain the unfolding politics and attempt to show that the government was still in command of events. That was to prove a very difficult task indeed. The ongoing votes in the House of Commons were to be inexplicable to all but the most clued-up of Westminster watchers. But it was also to be the Cabinet's divisions on the actual strategy that would be in plain sight for industry to see.

Around 9 p.m. on 15 January 2019, I dialled into one of those conference calls after having watched the vote live in the House of Commons on television at home. Vereker introduced the Chancellor Philip Hammond, Business Secretary Greg Clark and Brexit Secretary Steve Barclay. The call would do nothing to reassure the businesses who had dialled in from the UK or the many inward investors who had called from abroad. Hammond said that he was sure that a no-deal Brexit could be blocked, while also raising for the first time the possibility of a delay to Article 50. I had already got a whiff of that delay when the government had opted to extend the parliamentary timetable for debate well into January 2019 back in the previous summer. The Chancellor said the government would now seek to build a consensus in Parliament. 'We have to reach out to MPs in the Commons first', he said. 'It is clear there is a large majority in the Commons that is opposed to no-deal.'

Hammond also said the government would not put up any obstacles in the way of Nick Boles, the former Conservative minister who had been close to the entire David Cameron political project. Boles had proposed that the Commons Liaison Committee – made up of the chairs of the other select committees – could oversee attempts to find a way out of the impasse. He had been working with Labour MP Yvette Cooper and his former ministerial colleague Oliver Letwin on an amendment – the Cooper-Boles amendment – to delay Article 50 and effectively create a legislative block to a no-deal Brexit. To confuse business leaders further, the Prime Minister had made clear that she wanted to keep a no-deal exit on the table to press MPs into falling into line behind her deal. But Hammond and Clark attempted to reassure business leaders there was a majority in Parliament against a no-deal Brexit and that the Cooper-Boles amendment would provide a virtually guaranteed mechanism for MPs to block such a departure. It was a remarkable statement. It was the fact that it would not be the government itself but individual backbench MPs who would have to provide the mechanism to block a no-deal Brexit that most businesses were so concerned about!

In June 2019 I was to hear a further echo of this idea when Hammond threatened to vote for another parliamentary attempt to block no deal proposed by Letwin, only to be told by the then lame-duck Prime Minister that he would have to leave the government if he did so.

Steve Varley, chair of the management consultancy EY UK, who was on the conference call, sounded totally unconvinced by the reassurances around no deal: 'Based on advice from the Chancellor on a briefing call tonight we will continue to advise our clients to plan for a no-deal Brexit,' he told the *Financial Times* after the call had ended. I felt exactly the same.

Hammond also set out the sequencing by which Article 50 might be extended, delaying Brexit. The government was in no mood to consider 'unicorn' requests, he said. It felt like a substantial shift in the government's position on delaying Brexit: it sounded like ministers changing from no extension to extension. Hammond's words were, of course, firmly echoed by Greg Clark. However, to confuse businesses listening in even further, Steve Barclay struck a very different tone. He backed the Prime Minister's approach and suggested that he believed a harder Brexit approach could be a way to win round backbench Tory support. Barclay still wanted no-deal on the table as a way of being able to continue to negotiate with the EU. Business was hearing two very different approaches inside government, MPs were hearing two different approaches and the EU Commission could continue to see two different approaches.

Adam Marshall, head of the British Chambers of Commerce, spoke to the *Financial Times*'s Jim Pickard that evening and said: 'There are no more words to describe the frustration, impatience and growing anger among business after two-and-a-half years on a high-stakes political roller-coaster ride that shows no sign of stopping.' Others spoke to Pickard, including Stephen Phipson, chief executive of the EEF manufacturers' organisation, who said business was suffering from 'impossible uncertainty' because of 'Parliament's pantomime'. Carolyn Fairbairn, director general of the CBI, said companies believed that no deal was 'hurtling closer' with every passing day. 'A new plan is needed immediately. This is now a time for our politicians to make history as leaders.'

Pickard called me later that night and I told him it was vital that the government prevented a no-deal situation. 'No business wants to see this happen and government now needs to work with Parliament to ensure we rule this out and give business certainty,' I said in words which appeared in his *Financial Times* story the next day.[37]

The conference call between business leaders and executives lasted for only about fifty minutes. By the end of it, business was more confused than ever. Hammond said the government was still planning to use the Withdrawal Agreement as its central policy, while changing the Political Declaration which would guide future arrangements with the EU. Asked about a second referendum, the Chancellor warned that the last one took thirteen months from start to finish, there would be challenges in setting the question and it would be difficult given the European elections in May. Instead, the

---

37 Jim Pickard and Sarah Gordon, 'Hammond raises Article 50 delay to reassure business over Brexit', *Financial Times*, 16 January 2019.

priority was for Parliament to 'crystallise' its views. 'We need to understand where the weight of opinion of Parliament is,' he said. 'We now know what Parliament is against … we now need to understand what Parliament is for.'

Rather than clearing up the mess, the conference call had made matters worse. In the following twenty-four hours I took calls from across the business and political spectrum. It was clear that those at the very top of government were pulling the parliamentary strategy in different directions. There were to be more conference calls ahead and the mood was to darken yet further.

The following week, on 22 January, I was chairing a round-table on Brexit for the global fintech body Innovate Finance where I sit as a non-executive director. Outgoing Tory MEP Kay Swinburne was addressing the meeting on the likely politics ahead. It was a lively session. Many of the fintechs – like most other businesses – were finding planning very hard amid this ongoing this UK political soup.

In the middle of the meeting, I noted I had received a text message from BBC *Question Time* producer Poppy Bullard asking if I might be available to do the show that week. I felt a surge of adrenalin course through me. *Question Time* has one of the biggest audiences for any news show in the UK. Part of our approach at Cicero has been to eschew the cloak-and-dagger nature of some who lobby and to take our arguments right into the heart of the national debate. It has been a deliberate brand strategy for Cicero and a real point of difference for our business, and it is the reason we have recruited former broadcasters like Joey Jones and Kate McAndrew into our ranks, as they are both so good at taking the arguments public. I have always believed that you need to engage in a public conversation to lobby effectively in a digital world where your arguments are placed under more scrutiny than ever. It is probably the reason we named our business after a Roman orator!

Bullard had first contacted me on 25 June 2018 – the day my *Times* column on Boris Johnson's 'F**k business' comment had appeared – and had asked me then if I was happy to appear on the show at some time. I was genuinely thrilled and excited by the idea. I had been on standby a couple of times since the autumn of 2018 to appear, but Bullard thought this would be a good moment for me to come on to the programme to speak on behalf of the business sector. It seems to me putting together the *Question Time* panel is like some fiendishly complicated chess game. The production team doesn't just have to get a good mix of views – they also need to balance that with a range of personalities who might spark the debate together.

The next day Bullard called me back around lunchtime and confirmed they wanted me on the show. She asked me a series of questions about the issues of the day but the core topic would, of course, likely be Brexit. She told me this was unavoidable but that they hoped that the audience that week in Winchester would want to ask about a wide variety of other topics too, and I wanted to speak beyond Brexit. This would also be the third show hosted by its new presenter Fiona Bruce, who had replaced David Dimbleby after some twenty-five years in the chair. It was a big task fronting one of the most popular BBC One programmes and giving it a new feel and voice. A new chair would inevitably give *Question*

Time a reboot and Bruce would prove to do just that with her quiet authority, which allowed the panel rather than the presenter to be the centre of viewers' attention.

The previous week had been a particularly fractious affair when one of the guests – Labour's Diane Abbott – had engaged in a specular Twitter storm after the show about how she had been treated and how data about how Labour was polling among the electorate had been presented. Both the BBC and Fiona Bruce had been under siege on Twitter ever since. In fact, when I was announced on Twitter to be on the show only the night before, a whole bunch of social 'mud' was directed at all the panellists. It gave me some brief insight into the daily abuse that politicians and public figures face constantly on social media.

All the politicians who appear on the show get their researchers to prepare a detailed briefing on the location of the show, the other panellists' views and a gamed set of responses to the likely questions of the day. I wanted to prepare for this big moment thoroughly and asked colleagues in the Cicero team to prepare a comprehensive briefing for me. I could feel the excitement from my team as they sent it to me early the following morning.

On the same day I went into Parliament to meet Andrew Bowie for the first time in his new role as the Prime Minister's PPS. I was keen to know what arguments the government might have left to pass the deal and to understand them before I did the show. Maybe there was something they were holding in reserve, something that would be unveiled that would change hearts and minds. It still looked tough. Bowie met me in the heart of the Palace of Westminster in the Central Lobby and we walked across to the ornate Pugin Room, where many MPs take their guests to have a cup of tea (or something stronger). Determined to keep a clear head for the next twenty-four hours and my big TV appearance, I confined myself to some sparkling water. Bowie told me the approach from the PM was to remain resolute and work to convince more MPs to come onside. Many were calling it the 'one more heave' strategy.

Across the room I spotted Labour housing spokesman John Healey. Healey had also been booked to appear on *Question Time* with me that week. I went over to say hello and he admitted to me this was his first appearance on the show too – and he was equally nervous. *Question Time* is a big deal for politicians – it can make or break their careers – whereas the other guests like me would be able to speak their mind free of any party whip! I travelled home knowing it was not just me that would be on edge.

The night before the show I felt like a kid about to take his first exams. I could barely sleep, so, to stop my partner being disturbed, I slept in the spare bedroom so my racing mind would only interrupt one sleeping pattern that night. With barely three hours' sleep, I woke to the *Today* programme business slot around 6.15 a.m. and a stern warning from Airbus that Brexit was going to force the company to relocate some production from the UK if the political uncertainty was not going to come to an abrupt end. It was reported by some media that No. 10 had been working with Airbus to take the argument public in order to get MPs to focus minds on getting the deal over the line. Earlier that week James Dyson had also announced he was set to relocate his headquarters from the UK to Singapore. The backdrop for my appearance on the show was placed into even sharper relief. Businesses were making real-time decisions in the midst of the ongoing political paralysis. Sleep-deprived, my heart pounded and my adrenalin flowed just a little faster.

By total chance, I was chairing a conference that morning for one of our clients, the investment house WisdomTree. They had asked me to do a fireside chat on our current politics with my former political mentor and Chancellor Ken Clarke. The timing was perfect. Clarke now holds the distinction of being the guest with the most appearances on *Question Time*. So, before we went on stage together, I shared a cup of tea with a BBCQT maestro and picked his immense brains on how to tackle the show. Having briefed Clarke in the past in his own leadership campaign, he now briefed me! It felt good to see him. 'Just enjoy it,' he said. 'And remember to try and get them onside early in the programme.'

I also reached out that day to Siemens UK CEO Juergen Maier. Maier has also become a regular guest on the show as a voice of business. He had been in and around Downing Street and Parliament over the previous three years in order to try to secure a deal with the EU. The government had also commissioned him to lead the 'Made Smarter Review' on the digital economy. He told me: 'There is a warm-up question before the show gets recorded. Get the audience coming towards you if you can in that warm-up question.' It was truly great advice.

I spent the afternoon prepping with my Cicero colleagues Joey Jones and Tom Frackowiak, who put me through my paces. Beyond Brexit this was also the week when the Duke of Edinburgh would be involved in a spectacular road accident in his Land Rover near the Sandringham Estate in Norfolk. The Cicero team dug out some key insurance statistics for me about older versus younger drivers. I thought I had better come armed for the most likely non-Brexit question of the week.

I travelled down to Winchester from Waterloo. By now the adrenalin really was coursing faster than ever. In the space of a rail journey of only about an hour, I think I visited the toilet on board the train around three times! I arrived at the mighty Winchester Town Hall and was greeted by the production team. In the green room already were Healey and *Observer* columnist Sonia Sodha, who I had known from her time working with Ed Miliband. We greeted each other warmly and she admitted this was her first time on the show too! I felt even safer in those numbers surrounded by a group of *Question Time* newbies!

After some make-up (and another trip to the loo), I met the final two guests, LBC's morning show presenter Nick Ferrari and former Tory Brexit minister Suella Braverman. Braverman had also resigned in November 2018 from the government at the same time as her then boss Dominic Raab. It was going to be a punchy panel, I thought. On the way down to the hall where the audience was waiting, I must say Ferrari – as an old hand at such appearances – was very kind indeed and did most to put me at ease. Repeating Ken Clarke's refrain earlier that day, he said: 'Go for it and enjoy it.'

We waited outside the set as Fiona Bruce was introduced to the audience for only her third show. She walked onto the set and I and my fellow panellists could hear the roar of excitement and applause from the audience, who had been whipped into what could only be described as Jerry Springer levels of enthusiasm! Sonia Sodha and I looked at each other in dread. I was the last to be introduced and was greeted with a huge cheer. It all felt very weird – I don't think anyone in the audience knew me at all! By now my heart rate and my brain were on fire.

I sat down into my chair and the production team fixed my microphone and the make-up team applied a little more coverage. I was sat next to Suella Braverman, who I noted proceeded to open a very large briefing pack. On it were tens of Post-it notes with key phrases. It was an unusual briefing technique, but each to their own I thought. My one page of ideas looked rather paltry by comparison. Then we moved on to the warm-up question. I took the advice from Ken Clarke and Juergen Maier and managed to get a round of applause when answering the question, which was about an ISIS fighter who wanted to come back to the UK to face justice. I opposed the idea, and the audience applauded loudly! The warm-up was a really great idea. It lets your voice adjust to the room and allows you to build confidence. Fiona Bruce was brilliant at putting me at ease.

The music rolled and we were into the show itself, which is recorded around 8.30 p.m. to 9.30 p.m. that evening. I wanted to use the show as an opportunity to get the politicians to hear a business view and understand that business was finding planning ahead very difficult, as well as call for the country to come together. But first I had to make clear that in all my years around politics this was the most dismal parliament I had ever seen. The audience clearly felt the same way and applauded loudly again! I felt like I had landed my voice on this rather big stage. I went on: 'I'm in despair. We had a referendum. The country is very divided on the issue. I think the country remains very divided. But our politicians can't seem to work it out. Business is in despair. Our politicians need to come together.'

Suella Braverman, Nick Ferrari and I sparred on Airbus and Dyson. I think I caught the concerns of the audience about what Airbus had said earlier that day, but the others caught the mood of the room about Dyson – viewed as a great British entrepreneur, despite the relocation of his headquarters. Self-made business leaders who have created their enterprises resonate strongly with all voters. Dyson is just one of them. That's why the Vote Leave team had worked with them and not the corporates during the referendum. Halfway through the programme, the questions moved away from Brexit and you could feel the political tension in the room suddenly lift.

A young student spoke powerfully about the severe lack of mental health services on offer in the UK. Having seen members of my own family unable to get mental health services directly from the NHS, I felt able to speak out on the subject. After the show the producers told me that the segment of the show had been the most popular in some time. I was also able to give a shout-out to my work with both Stonewall, which helps so many LGBT people with mental health issues, and also to Robert Peston's brilliant Speakers4Schools initiative, which sends businesses leaders into schools to talk about their lives and careers. (And, in case you were wondering, I did get asked about the Duke of Edinburgh's driving abilities too!)

Earlier in January I had been speaking to 250 thirteen-year-olds at a school in Doncaster as part of Speakers4Schools. While *Question Time* was exciting, speaking to the children was just as terrifying. They asked such brilliant questions. One of them had asked me: 'How do you look after your own mental health?' Wow, I thought, that is a question I would never have been able to ask or even have thought about when I was thirteen. I really wanted to tell that story and I'm glad I managed to do so to the almost four million people who watch *Question Time* each week.

The day after *Question Time* was broadcast, I received an email from the headmaster of the Doncaster school where I had spoken. The note came out of the blue and read: 'I can't tell you how much you mentioning the mental health question has meant to a young thirteen-year-old girl. That someone listened to her – answered her question – and raised the issue on BBC *Question Time* on the national stage.' I have kept that email. I have printed it out and I will treasure it for ever. In the midst of all the lobbying for businesses over Brexit, that note means more than any other.

17

ENDGAMES

After the largest defeat in UK parliamentary history and the further defeats to follow, most businesses started to tune out from politics by February and March 2019. There really was no lobbying to be done by then. They were far more focused on getting ready for a hard exit on 29 March. Business did not really warm to the Withdrawal Agreement or the future Political Declaration but – with the clock ticking away – there was no other negotiation in place with the EU to secure transition.

My team and I had spent the previous two years regularly briefing boardrooms on the political machinations. By the time the Prime Minister's deal went down to another landslide defeat on 12 March 2019, there was only political risk analysis that they cared about. The situation had actually been the same for months before then. All companies wanted to do was keep tabs on the risk of a crash-out Brexit.

By the middle of February, British politics had hit a quagmire and there appeared to be no way out of the morass. No. 10 rolled out another series of conference calls to try to calm the business community down. It wasn't working very well.

The calls didn't really give business any more information that they couldn't already read from the incessant leaking emanating from each and every Cabinet meeting. By the time you had dialled into the conference call, you had pieced together much of the Cabinet's war of words in briefings – some of which I had already sent to some of the businesses dialling in. This was supplemented by reading the frenzied scribbling on the machinations of Brexit in *The Times*, *Daily Telegraph* and *Financial Times* with a smattering of the excellent London Playbook morning briefing from Politico's Jack Blanchard for good measure.

On 12 February 2019 I had dialled into another call – this time with the Prime Minister. This time there was to be no equivocation on the government's stance on no deal. Despite the attempt to bring the ERG on board, her words were designed to appease a nervous business community that could only see what some ministers were still saying in public – to keep no deal on the table. She offered some sense of the intense talks still talking place with Tory MPs and with the EU Commission, as well as an attempt to reach out to Jeremy Corbyn. She told us:

> We are going flat out to reach a deal that Parliament can accept. We want a deal. We can only get a deal if Parliament will accept it. We are negotiating with the EU to ensure we get legally binding changes. I have been talking to MPs in depth across all parties focusing on workers' rights and the role for Parliament.

Over three months later towards the endgame of the May

premiership the same ideas were being rolled out to try and get Labour MPs on board, but to no avail. Her chief of staff Gavin Barwell even invited Labour MPs to meet him the week she resigned – but few actually turned up, sensing the power draining away from No. 10.

No one sounded very positive when asking questions on this latest business call. In fact, business leaders told May and Vereker directly that they were now ramping up their plans for no deal. No time left. No delay possible. The months of February, March and early April 2019 were supposedly about Parliament taking back control from the government in a series of what looked like clearly coordinated moves with Speaker Bercow. But, in the end, there was little to see here either for business. The machinations were to no avail. There was intense focus on the so-called indicative votes to try and smoke out what Parliament actually did want to approve. The votes looked at everything from formally requesting no deal to a customs union or a Norway-style option, but no single idea carried the day. There was immense tiredness and paralysis in the political system.

I and my Cicero colleagues Joey Jones and Nikki da Costa found ourselves shuttling back and forward to the 'tented media village' on College Green outside Parliament, trying to decipher the madness going on in the building across the road. Just before the second defeat of the Prime Minister's deal, I was waiting to go on air on BBC News and arrived a little early. I climbed up to the BBC gantry, which was on scaffolding on the Green. All the main broadcasters – BBC, ITN and Sky – had spent a fortune on these gantries which were to become a permanent fixture of the political scene for almost five months from November 2018 to Easter 2019. They were built up high to try to outflank the Brexit protestors on both sides with their banners. In the end the protestors outwitted the broadcasters by buying long poles to raise their placards to the height of the gantries. You could not make it up – such was the madness of our politics by then. By the time the gantries were taken down over Easter 2019 the grass underneath was as exhausted as the politicians' words.

I prepared for my interview and the line I wanted to take. By that stage I was simply desperate, like the rest of business, for the political logjam to end and called for MPs to get together and compromise to find a deal. Being interviewed before me was the former Brexit minister and Tory MP David Jones, who was now one of the leading lights of the ERG. He got himself into position in front of the cameras. As he did, DUP Brexit spokesman Sammy Wilson climbed up the steps and onto the gantry. He was to be interviewed after me. I watched as Jones spotted Wilson and gave him a long wink, of the kind that could only mean the DUP was firmly in cahoots with the ERG on both their message spin and voting operation. I kept that moment in my mind. The DUP would have willingly voted for the Norway option, just like the SNP. This position was so far away from the ERG philosophy. Politics was totally out of sorts.

In an interview on talkRADIO a few days later I dubbed the ERG 'the DUP's useful idiots' in the process, such was my frustration. It was my sense that the DUP would have been very happy with a close alignment with the EU. I didn't stay on the line to listen in to the next interview with the ERG

MP Mark Francois, who was apparently so irate he sounded as if he was about to explode!

I had received intense lobbying from some Tory MPs to get business to back that so-called Norway option. I was briefly attracted to it myself as a way of breaking the deadlock. In December 2018, before the vote on the Prime Minister's deal was pulled, I had invited Nick Boles, then a Tory MP, to come and talk to a range of businesses about the plan. Nick and the then Treasury Select Committee chair Nicky Morgan MP had been the leading proponents of the idea. Boles made clear he was not set to introduce the idea into the House of Commons until Theresa May's deal was defeated. He said: 'We have to do this in order and I will support the PM until it is clear her deal will fail.'

At the end of 2018, the campaign for Norway was in full swing. But business was split. In the case of some US organisations passporting currently through London, it was a no-brainer to back Norway as an idea. They could happily live with being a rule taker (they already were rule takers in many ways), and it would allow them to keep their foothold in the UK and passport as part of the EEA. However, for many UK domestic businesses a Norway model just wasn't an option, as they had constructed their business in a very different way. They also operated in the context of a UK government and UK Parliament alone as their key interlocutor for EU laws and so feared being shut out of the decision making. So, getting business to speak as one on Norway just wasn't going to happen.

By the middle of March, the UK government launched its plans for tariffs in case of a no-deal scenario on 29 March. If people were nervous before, the jumpiness went up another level. Another conference call was hastily convened on 13 March with Business Secretary Greg Clark, Department for International Trade minister George Hollingbery and Treasury financial secretary and paymaster general Mel Stride – technically the nation's chief tax collector.

By the time of this call, the government was now set to announce an extension to Article 50 and to push this through in the House of Commons despite huge opposition from the Tory benches. The next day we were indeed to witness the bizarre spectacle of Brexit Secretary Steve Barclay proposing the legislation to extend Article 50 at the ministerial despatch box in the Chamber, before promptly walking into the No lobby and voting against the measure he had proposed! Trying to explain what was going on inside government and Parliament by then had really become futile. Business Secretary Greg Clark told the businesses on the conference call line the day before:

I will vote for an extension to make sure there is no damage to our economy. We need to end the uncertainty which is damaging to business. The parliamentary process will now start to look at options and put in train a set of steps that will ensure we don't leave in a disorderly way. There will be a rapid conclusion on our future relationship with the EU.

Reading those words back at time of writing this book in mid-2019, it is hardly a wonder that business felt no confidence in government given what was to come, despite all of Clark's efforts. Hollingbery then laid out the approach towards the tariff regime the government was set to put in place if Parliament had voted to block an extension and in favour of a crash-out. He said: 'We have thought long and hard about the industries we need to protect. We have balanced the need to protect consumers alongside the impact of a rapid change for some businesses. This will be a temporary measure and we will review in one year.'

Mel Stride then spoke. He told us:

All goods will need to be declared using the existing EU customs code – apart for special arrangements for Northern Ireland. On the Northern Ireland border the customs tariff will be unapplied at that border – and there will be no physical infrastructure at the border. The UK government will not chase down non-high-risk goods – there will be no checks or controls on goods to Northern Ireland from Ireland.

The realities of months and months of wrangling over the Northern Ireland border and backstop were to be met with a really lax set of customs procedures by the UK. Dialling into the call was a host of Northern Ireland business leaders who had real concerns about the applicability of the plans.

By the time MPs had voted to reject the Withdrawal Agreement again on 29 March by 344 votes to 286 – the very day the UK was supposed to leave the EU – business was simply doing its own thing. I now reflect that the UK economy has been kept running through this period by the actions of business rather than our politicians.

Following the parliamentary vote to extend the Article

50 process later into 2019, the UK government and the EU Commission agreed to hold an emergency summit in Brussels on 10 April in order to provide the UK with more time to approve the Withdrawal Agreement. This was to be the final roll of the dice for Theresa May. She had wanted a short extension to the end of June to allow the UK Parliament time to ratify the deal and to ensure that the UK would not have to elect new MEPs to sit in the European Parliament in elections, which would only be horrendous for her own governing party.

However, EU Council President Donald Tusk and German Chancellor Angela Merkel were less convinced and believed the UK and the EU institutions would need more time to pass the deal. President Macron of France had really had enough of the Brexit impasse by then and believed that a short extension to June would be a better political outcome, but he was persuaded to drop his opposition to a longer extension. The summit closed and the UK was given until 31 October to pass the deal unless it could do so earlier in May. EU premiers did not want to keep coming back for emergency summits on Brexit. In the meantime, the UK would have to elect those new MEPs. At the start of 2019, no one in Brussels or in London had thought that was a viable option.

The politics just drifted on. And the business conference calls with No. 10 just rolled on but to no avail, creating no more clarity. What could the politicians actually say? On 11 April, before the House of Commons rose for its Easter break following the EU summit (there were some asking why MPs were taking any time away from sorting the national crisis) No. 10 organised another call, this time hosted by Business

Secretary Greg Clark and Environment Secretary Michael Gove. It was to prove to be the most fractious yet with business leaders, and indeed the last major business phone call of the May premiership.

Clark started by saying he hoped that MPs would ratify the deal before 22 May and that the UK would not then have to take part in the European Parliament elections – an idea that most politicians, commentators and businesses had thought was 'fantasy politics'. He added: 'We are preparing for the EU elections. The UK will continue to be a good member of the EU. We have a duty of "sincere cooperation". Leaving without a deal will *not* happen and there is a sense of relief that we now have until 31 October.' For many on the call, the feeling was not one of relief but one of purgatory.

Gove then spoke. It was perhaps his most business-friendly set of comments since before the Brexit referendum itself. He told us: 'We recognise the current situation causes uncertainty. We don't want the expense of the EU elections and we want to give business certainty. We are working with Labour right now and have shared documents with them.' In a final nod of encouragement, he told us: 'There will be a deal – I firmly believe the UK will get its own bespoke deal with the EU.'

The government had been locked in fruitless talks with the Labour Party for weeks which seemed to be going nowhere. The Labour front bench knew that power was seeping away from the Prime Minister and had no interest in helping her get her Brexit deal over the line. It was brutal, but it was raw politics.

After months and months of wrangling, Gove indicated he believed the UK might be able to still strike a bespoke arrangement with the EU. When it came to questions the business leaders were incredulous, and some of them could not even hide their anger. One major US manufacturer on the call said: 'We have had months and months of promises and expectations from all of you. None of it has come to pass. I don't have any trust left and I am making plans for my business accordingly.'

'No trust left' – the words were jarring and summed up the situation perfectly. Any morsel of trust between business and government had gone. I had never heard a business leader talk to senior government ministers in that way, at any time, let alone in front of everyone else who had dialled in. I wrote those words down on my pad. I had to look at them again and again; it was remarkable. The endgame for the May government was approaching. But business had already got there. Neither side was listening to the other.

One of the business leaders dialling in to that call spoke to me for this book and said: 'Theresa May has had no EQ throughout this entire process. And certainly no EQ to listen to business.' The die had been cast for many businesses in the summer of 2016 when they had been shut out of the discussion. Despite all the efforts of the Prime Minister and her team to secure that soft landing, Parliament would not play ball and business had ceased to do any lifting at all.

Easter recess in 2019 came as a blessed relief to everyone. More exhaustion – more failed promises. I spent the Easter week in Perthshire, unwinding with my family. When I returned from the break, I had a meeting booked in Downing Street to see the business liaison team.

As I walked up Downing Street, I could see the Cabinet

had been summoned for another emergency 'what to do next' meeting. But support for the Prime Minister was draining away. I really didn't get the sense that many of them wanted to help her any more; they were helping themselves to climb into her chair. I entered through the famous black door and sat down in the waiting area just off the main entrance hall. I already knew my meeting would be running late. Sat in the waiting room you can hear the old grandfather clock ticking. The sounds of the clock appeared to be particularly loud that morning. There was an eerie silence in the building that is the centre of our government. I watched as the clock struck 11 a.m. precisely and Michael Gove sped through the hallway to get to the Cabinet meeting in his usual punctilious way. I then watched in disbelief as various other Cabinet members walked in at five past, ten past and quarter past the hour. Around a third of the Cabinet had arrived late or very late for the meeting.

It was clear to me by then that No. 10 had no grip on proceedings. The centre could not hold. But the most significant thing was the fact that, for business, the deadline of 29 March had been breached. A feeling of never-never land had descended on our politics. For business it was to last until the arrival of a new Prime Minister – and beyond.

18

A NEW GAME?

The final days of 'May' were the saddest sight. Perhaps the end really had been inevitable for weeks. I had very mixed feelings. Knowing what I had been told about the Prime Minister's desire to secure transition for our economy and a deal with the EU made me feel natural human sympathy for her. Having been told back in the summer of 2016 that she wanted to ensure no economic dislocation for the country made me agree with the sentiment – she had 'done her best'.

But the sphinx-link behaviour in Downing Street had done her no favours and the way in which business had been shut out for much of her premiership was hard to forgive. The fact also that 'her deal' (as her Cabinet would always describe it with one eye on her job throughout the negotiations themselves) with the EU had gone down to the largest defeat in parliamentary history in January 2019 meant there was nothing that was going to change the seemingly inevitable demise by the late spring. The 'one more heave' strategy in Parliament had signally failed on two more occasions. The newspapers had already planned to call time on her premiership months earlier, her supply and confidence partner the

DUP was resolute in its opposition to the backstop and the ERG 'party within a party' had been agitating for her entire premiership to remove her.

I have little doubt that there would have been a May polling 'bounce' if she had secured her deal and left the EU on time. Her Chancellor Philip Hammond said there would have been an economic bounce too. Most businesses thought the same. But as we all endured the torture of the parliamentary votes of January to March 2019, the bounce failed to materialise. The pound, which had been the economic barometer of Brexit since 2016, turned south once again.

This depressing backdrop for our economy was also reflected in the mood in Downing Street, which most insiders described to me in May and June as 'eerily silent'. I had noted this myself in my visits over that period where power seemed to have totally drained away, even in the period before the Prime Minister resigned. That day in April when I had watched around a third of the Cabinet arrive late for its meeting told me all I needed to know. In fact, by then all the major candidates to replace the Prime Minister were on overt manoeuvres to do just that.

Around the same time, I took a call from a former Tory MP who was working behind the scenes on one of the putative Tory leadership campaigns. He sounded me out about whether I wanted to get involved and potentially run the communications effort. We talked a couple of times and met in Westminster but there was not a lot to think about. It had been almost twenty years since I had worked with Ken Clarke on his leadership bids. A lot of water had flowed under the political bridge since then. I needed to know the candidate wanted to secure transition for the economy, but I didn't hear those words. Ultimately, that candidate never threw his hat into the already crowded ring. The candidacy was a rather fantastical idea in itself. The ring was already filled with candidates who really were wanting to raise their profiles to get a future Cabinet role under the new Tory leader or who were laying down markers for a future leadership bid, with some gaming that they would not have long to wait.

Over the summer of 2019 it was very difficult for business to listen in to the Tory leadership campaign, which was defined by how hard the approach to Brexit might be. It felt like we had gone back in time to the debates of the summer of 2016 in the immediate aftermath of the referendum. It was as if the previous three years, with all the political torture for MPs, for business and for voters, had simply never happened.

Of course, the Tory 'selectorate', of around 160,000 members, mainly wanted to hear very different notes chimed to the interests of business. Any time a candidate suggested that a no-deal Brexit should be taken off the table, the political odds with the selectorate seemed to turn against them. In the early part of the leadership election, like most of the country, I found myself listening to Rory Stewart much more than any of the other candidates, with the exception of Boris Johnson. His campaign was perhaps the most interesting of all. His quirky, idiosyncratic approach to the leadership election caught some media fire. From my perspective as a communications guy, his Twitter 'walks' around the country were a brilliant blend of old-style political hustings brought into the twenty-first century – but liberal Twitter was not the audience he needed to reach in a Tory leadership poll.

Stewart's message about avoiding a no-deal Brexit was perhaps the one which most businesses felt most comfortable with. But, of course, it wasn't going to win the day. Some even joked that his campaign was brilliant to become the leader of another party, so far from his position had the Tory selectorate travelled over the previous two decades. Business therefore focused in on the comments of the front-runner, Boris Johnson, whose script on the economics had been reset. Speaking at his campaign launch on 12 June 2019, Johnson said: 'I was just about the only politician who [as London mayor] was willing to stick up for financial services ... we are willing to encourage the tech wizards and the shopkeepers and the taxi drivers and, yes, the bankers as well.'[38]

Throughout his campaign launch, Mr Johnson was at pains to express support for business and financial services, in particular, arguing that entrepreneurship was essential if the UK was to fund public services. He dismissed his 'F**k business' comments of the past as 'plaster' that falls off the ceiling when he is trying to catch the attention of the nation. But the new notes being chimed were welcome to hear. The *Financial Times* noted at the time:

For corporate Britain, Mr Johnson's tone will probably be welcomed after the cold shoulder Mrs May appeared to give business for much of her premiership. However, many business people will remember that last year, as foreign secretary, Mr Johnson said 'F**k business', and he

---

38 James Blitz, 'Five key quotes from Boris Johnson's Tory leadership campaign launch', *Financial Times*, 12 June 2019.

could well pursue a no-deal Brexit that risks major economic damage.[39]

The question on the minds of most business leaders was: how will all the candidates adapt their campaigning poetry to Tory MPs and members into the prose of running a government? Would they pivot? During the early summer of 2019, that was the essential question being posed by business: should we be preparing for a hard Brexit now? Has the likelihood of a no-deal outcome just gone through the roof? Would Parliament block the prospects of no deal? If so, will we face an early general election? Will that election be of Boris Johnson's or Parliament's choosing? Will it come before or after 31 October?

As time ticked on, for business the concept of the transitional period really had become that 'withering asset'. The agreement with the EU negotiated by Theresa May only secured a transition until December 2020. The clock was ticking on that offer in the same way it ticked on Britain's wider negotiations. I sat down with the chief lobbyist of one of the biggest names in the City in mid-June 2019. She told me:

We have effectively disbanded our Brexit steering group. There is nothing more to do. We were ready for 29 March – as we were told to be by our regulator – by ensuring we could access the EU passport regardless of the outcome of the politics. We are ready, we have moved on in every sense.

---

39 James Blitz, 'Five key quotes from Boris Johnson's Tory leadership campaign launch', *Financial Times*, 12 June 2019.

Around the same time, speaking at *The Times* business summit in mid-June 2019, Aston Martin CEO Andy Palmer described the then current state of British politics for business as a kind of 'purgatory'.[40] He was right. That's how most people felt. But some businesspeople – who were closer to party politics themselves – thought there might be a chance to break out of the paralysis. The most notable was Michael Spencer, the self-made City titan who had backed Remain, but by now really wanted the country to move on, like so many of us. He had been an early backer of David Cameron in 2005 and served as his party treasurer, bankrolling support for the party.

The closeness between the Conservatives and corporate funders is well known. Without that support the Tories would – literally – not be in business. Labour's union paymasters bankroll the party with eye-watering sums. But Brexit and the political paralysis had destroyed the Tories' fundraising abilities by the first quarter of 2019. Income from wealthy tycoons plunged in the first three months of 2019. Grim figures from the Electoral Commission showed the Tories received £3.7 million from 220 donors between January and March 2019, half of the £7.5 million from 230 donors in the final quarter of 2018. It was the Tories' smallest quarterly total since the final three months of 2017. The largest donor in those three months had been Sir Mick Davis, a mining millionaire who also happened to be the Tories' Treasurer and chief executive. He reached into his own pocket to give £315,980. He resigned the day Boris Johnson became Prime Minister.

Speaking to the Radio 4 *Today* programme in mid-June 2019,

---

40 '*Times* CEO Summit 2019: Quotes from the day', *The Times*, 12 June 2019.

Michael Spencer talked about the fact he had donated to a range of the leadership campaigns from Dominic Raab to Sajid Javid to Boris Johnson. Asked why a businessman who had backed Remain had donated to Boris Johnson's campaign, he said: 'He said ["F**k business"] but he probably didn't mean it – he was frustrated.' Just as City titans Martin Gilbert and John McFarlane had earlier told me for this book, they believed that Boris Johnson's true colours were actually much more pro-business than Theresa May's.

Spencer was articulating what many pro-business Conservatives felt with their heads and also their hearts. They had voted to remain in the EU, were in a minority in the Tory Party and then lost the referendum itself. A few had backed a referendum on the final deal, but it appeared neither Parliament nor the electorate really wanted to have another go at this debate which was continuing the deep divisions in the country. The Remainer camp had failed to convince enough people pre- and post-referendum – Deborah Mattinson's detailed polling made that clear enough.

So the only way to be able to leave was to try another Prime Minister with a different approach, one who would be able to better 'sell' their deal to Tory MPs and to the electorate. In politics, as in business, you can have the most detailed plans and great ideas, but they are useless unless you can sell them. Theresa May had many qualities, but sales was not part of her toolkit. The signs were good in that Boris Johnson was reaching out to business and the City investors in order to quell their concerns about his approach. Unlike May who had stepped away from business, it appeared a new Conservative leader was going to try to bring them onside.

One of his first appointments to No. 10 was Sky executive Andrew Griffith to replace Vereker as chief business adviser. Martin Gilbert, who sat on the Sky board, told me: 'He is a good guy and business will like him.' Within days, Griffith was engaging with Britain's business leaders and clearly hungry for ideas. Similarly pro-enterprise ministers like Sajid Javid as Chancellor and Liz Truss as Secretary of State for International Trade always want to lean towards business, and that is what most involved in commerce will want to hear.

But the new Boris Johnson administration was to look very different from Theresa May's. There were few former Remainer Tories being invited into a 'big tent' style of leadership. One of those ministers under May who did find themselves in the first Boris Johnson Cabinet said to me: 'In the end I decided it was better to be in the same car as Boris – guiding him in the right direction.'

Time will tell whether or not that approach will work. The idea of a back-seat driver has not been good for previous Tory premiers, and nor has the idea of them trying to grab the steering wheel while someone is driving. But, after almost four years of political turmoil, what is clear is that a new approach is needed.

All new ministers in the Johnson administration had to sign up to a political pledge to leave the EU on 31 October 2019 with or without a deal. They could be in no doubt now about the approach in the first phase of the Johnson government – a phase which in its first fifty days proved to be politically explosive.

PERORATION – BUSINESS AND POLITICS FROM HERE?

As I had called our business Cicero, I couldn't resist the idea of a peroration rather than a conclusion to this book. A peroration ends a great piece of rhetoric. But I hope you feel this has been an easier journey than listening to a six- or seven-hour speech! Thank you for joining me on this journey of the most exciting, exhilarating and exhausting time in my professional life. I hope you can empathise. Frankly, most of the people who might be even vaguely interested in reading this book were probably feeling the same in the summer of 2019.

As we wait and see if the approach of a new Prime Minister is going to reset relations with the EU for better or worse, I am also interested to see if the Tory Party – of which I have been a member for the past thirty-five years, for which I have deep affection and in which I have made deep friendships – is going to be able to also reset its relations with business too.

That has been the locus of this book. I am not a reporter or a TV political editor but a lobbyist, and in these pages I have been interested in whether the relationship can be fixed or if

4649

---

it is broken for good. Of course, much of the answer to these questions depends on breaking out of the Brexit purgatory, but if we are able to do that, what might a more evenly balanced relationship look like now?

Let me start by taking the words of two now former PPSs to the Prime Minister, who have been close to the heart of power in the past decade. Sam Gyimah had been David Cameron's PPS and later resigned from Theresa May's government; he subsequently attempted to stand for his party's leadership on a pro-referendum ticket to – inevitably – very little avail. But Gyimah has an insight which I think is worth listening to. He told me: 'The Tory Party's compass has been scrambled and it does not know how to point north any more. It has wanted to be a low-tax and low-regulation party while at the same time it has attacked wealth creation.' Meanwhile, Andrew Bowie, who had been PPS to Theresa May over her last tumultuous six months in power, told me: 'The Conservative Party has for a while lost its common-sense pragmatism and it needs to get it back and quickly.'

This view was echoed more widely on the Tory benches by more centre-right politicians. Amber Rudd told me for this book: 'We need to move on from this moment and we need to roll our sleeves up and work together with and not against business.' In a nod to what she wanted to see in British political and business life, she told me: 'I think business needs to see more charisma from its business leaders. We need strong leaders who can capture the public imagination. We also need the same thing from our political leaders too.'

One of the scarring effects of the previous few years has been the concern from business that it is not being listened to and cannot take a part in the wider public debates like Brexit which are shaping society. When David Cameron's communications chief Craig Oliver told me – as noted earlier in this book – that the real concern in the Cameron government was that business would just not be active enough in the debate, I told him that business had been burnt by the experiences of the previous decade when it had chosen to speak out. Of course, Oliver was right and remains right. In order for business to play a legitimate part in a democratic society, it needs to speak up and be part of the national conversation. Right now, it has a tendency to 'pop up' when it wants something and to keep its head down at all other times. It can hardly then wonder why politicians and the public have become so sceptical of business intentions. For me, it needs to play an active and ongoing part in the discussion on the future of our country.

Juergen Maier makes this very point. He says:

Of course business needs to speak up. It needs to play an active part in society. Business does not have a choice about getting involved. There are a whole number of issues around technology and work for example that can only be addressed by business and politics working together. But trust has broken down right now. Business and politicians must work harder at fixing that. I'm not seeing enough appetite from politicians to invest in manufacturing or infrastructure or tech to fire up the fourth industrial revolution.

But for me the problem has been about politicians and businesses just not listening to each other over the last few years, or at least taking on board each other's ideas. I spoke to one of my longest-standing clients about this very subject. Jon Whitehouse is the head of government relations at Barclays Bank. Given Barclays' role in the wider economy, he is in and out of Parliament all the time, speaking to both the government and opposition parties. Whether his boss is meeting the UK Prime Minister or the President of the United States, Whitehouse's job is to keep the dialogue going at all times – to keep the door open in good times and bad. Speaking to me for this book, he told me: 'The problem in the past few years has been the dialogue itself. Things can only really improve from this point.'

I have to reflect as I conclude that some of the major business representative bodies have misfired badly during this whole Brexit period. Rather than be seen to listen to how the electorate had voted, they carried on with clarion calls for things which would not be politically realistic. Making an argument solely based on an economic case and not a wider societal one is destined to fall flat on its face in an age disorientated by globalisation and digitalisation. You might say that 'values signalling' has more political power right now than economics. But one person I believe has made the arguments more cogently, and who only resorted to the loudest lobbying megaphone when really necessary, has been Adam Marshall, the British Chambers of Commerce director general. I have no brief for Marshall at all, but I believe he has listened more than talked to the politics of our times. Marshall agrees wholeheartedly with Whitehouse and points towards a fundamental reframing of the way that government and business needs to talk to one another. He told me:

The UK needs a more open and frank dialogue between government and business and one that endures – regardless of changes in ministers or political control. We need fewer ideological volleys and more deep, constructive work on the details that determine whether our country succeeds or stagnates. The countries I most admire use that dialogue to respond quickly to changes in global commercial decisions, technology and geopolitics – and put the right incentives in place to get business investing and growing.

I could not have put it better myself. At the time of writing, I understand that the UK Cabinet Secretary Mark Sedwill is working on that very idea. He wants to create a better, deeper long-term relationship and dialogue between business and government, which the UK now sorely needs. I hope his thinking will hit the in-tray of our new Prime Minister Boris Johnson and become a real political priority. That really will be the way to repudiate the idea 'F**k business'.

Of course, any new settlement and a new agenda between business and politics requires business itself to step up and recognise its own failings. The whole debate about purpose in business is very valuable to this discussion. As Helena Morrissey put it: 'We need more humility from business.' She is spot on. We are simply not going to reconnect politics and business together by just wishing it. Commerce needs to lean in to the future conversations and come up with solutions that reflect political realities. That is not about bowing to populism; far from it – it is about embracing a way of doing business that genuinely supports the communities in which firms operate.

One of the books which has greatly influenced my thinking in the past decade is *Connect: How Companies Can Connect by Radically Engaging with Society*. It was written by former BP CEO Lord (John) Browne, McKinsey consultant Robin Nuttall and tech entrepreneur Tommy Stadlen. Since the book was published in the mid-2010s, I have got to know Stadlen well. We meet as often as we are able and we regularly talk together in person or on digital platforms about the challenges in business and how it is often simply failing to connect with the new societal challenges we face. Stadlen tells me:

> Great companies are fuelled by purpose, more than capital and good ideas. The great social burdens of our time from climate change to obesity cannot be solved by government alone. We need business and innovation to solve those challenges. Government and society cannot afford to shut enterprise out of the debate, however great the populist urge to do so.

In the US, the political and business debate seems to take a different form. While in recent times in the UK the politicians want to show that they put the voters' interests ahead of business, in the US business is listened to a lot more. Despite the financial crisis starting in the US, it appears the American body politic has moved faster to get business and politics working together. Some will tell you that's because 'money talks' there. Of course, to a large extent that's true, and I don't want to see a system develop in this country where the size of your campaign donation dictates whether or not your arguments land with the political class, or where you only get to meet a politician by opening a cheque book. That is a truly rotten idea and we should remain vigilant in this country to ensure it never takes over.

However, in the US there is a wider connection being made between business and society. With a businessman – of sorts – in the White House, and with activist business leaders like former Starbucks CEO Howard Schultz and Facebook CEO Mark Zuckerberg entering the political arena in recent times, there appears to be more acceptance of the need for business leaders to play their part in solving fundamental social and environmental issues. How would UK politicians react to business leaders stepping on their patch? Right now – not well. They would be told to take their ball away and play somewhere else.

But business also needs to be frank with itself. A large part of the reason why it has been shut out of the debates in the last decade is a direct result of the financial crisis, excessive executive pay and the impact of austerity. Big finance in particular is still seen as part of the problem and not the solution, despite all the hard work being done by the financial services sector to get the UK economy moving again to some success. Labour frontbencher Jonathan Reynolds told me: 'The core problem is the economy. The proportion of economic returns flowing to capital rather than to labour has been increasing since the 1970s. That imbalance must be addressed.' But he admits that Labour also need to start talking much more about wealth creation, both to business that is running scared of Corbyn and McDonnell and also to voters themselves. 'People need to see their savings going directly towards something that will help their lives and their families,' he says. Regardless of your politics, he is right about that. A more visceral connection between economics and society is the only way forward to sort the 'F**k business' sentiment.

Laura Kuenssberg tells me: 'The relationship between business and politics won't reboot until living standards and wages rise. It means we might have to wait for another generation of leaders in politics and business for that relationship to improve.' Having observed business and politics in the last decade, I am certain she is right, too.

Our country is turning yet another page in its politics. I hope that in this book I have been able to provide you with a glimpse into the state of both business and politics. My purpose in writing this book, as I said at the outset, is not as an academic tome or a management textbook, but reflections on the journey our businesses have been on with our politicians. My earnest hope is that it will not have to wait for a new generation of leaders to bridge the gulf between business and politics in this country. I hope that our politics can set us back on the right track to working together for the common good very soon.

ACKNOWLEDGEMENTS

I want to thank the many people who have given their time and energy to my writing this book, including my Cicero colleagues, as well as everyone listed here who spoke to me in the spring and early summer of 2019:

Geoff Aberdein, Omar Ali, Andrew Bailey, Burkhard Balz, Steve Barclay, Inga Beale, Andrew Bowie, Robert Buckland, Miles Celic, Nikki da Costa, Chris Cummings, Paul Drechsler, Alastair Evans, David Frost, Martin Gilbert, John Godfrey, Sam Gyimah, Richard Harrington, Mark Hoban, Luigi Ippolito, Rachel Kent, Laura Kuenssberg, Juergen Maier, Adam Marshall, Christian May, John McFarlane, Jimmy McLoughlin, Nicky Morgan, Dame Helena Morrissey, Craig Oliver, George Parker, Barney Reynolds, Jonathan Reynolds, Neale Richmond, Amber Rudd, Andy Silvester, David Singleton, Tommy Stadlen, Liz Truss, Shriti Vadera, Jon Whitehouse.

ABOUT THE AUTHOR

© Maxwell Poth

IAIN ANDERSON is the founder and chairman of Cicero Group, the UK's largest independent lobbying business. He has over twenty-five years' experience in communications, initially as a business journalist and then as a founding shareholder at Incisive Media. He has also worked for a range of politicians, including the Rt Hon. Kenneth Clarke MP on his leadership bids. Iain focuses on strategy, supporting many global FTSE and Fortune 500 blue-chip organisations. He regularly contributes to national and international print and broadcast media including Sky News and BBC. He is one of the *Financial Times*/OUTstanding Global 100 Executives and a Freeman of the City of London and is immensely proud to be a Stonewall ambassador. He lives in London and is a tennis geek, an Arsenal season ticket holder and an opera nut.

INDEX